# German Awakening

*Tales from an American Life*

## Amy Hallberg

Wise Ink Creative Publishing

## Part Three: Weiterleben / Living On

## Part Four: Nachspiel / Postlude

# PART ONE

# Wanderschaft / Journey

1973–1990

# I

## Learning to Read / Lesen lernen

My mother always told me not to go around reading, or I would learn something. That's how I learned about subtext. Our eyes would meet in secret rebellion, her brows arched with the hint of a smile, head tipped just so. We repeated this private ritual every time I mentioned something I'd read.

"What did I tell you about reading?" Mom demanded, as if arming her lookalike daughter with an unspoken challenge: educate yourself.

She herself read slowly. Deliberately. She needed silence to make the connection between letters and words. Mom spoke of long nights as a child, practicing spelling lists. How her own mom promised to buy her a puzzle for any perfect spelling test. Grandma told perfect strangers that her older two daughters were smart. But Katy—my mom—was the pretty one. I heard this story from both my aunts and my mom. In Mom's version, she only ever got three puzzles in all that time. I suspect she worked hardest for the other reward: after they finished studying, Mom and Grandma would nestle in a chair and recite poetry by lamplight.

Mom's story always ended with the same proclamation: "But you're like my sisters. You're good at language." She would beam, relieved I'd escaped her curse. "As a tiny girl, you sat in shopping carts and read the labels aloud."

I don't remember that part. I recall the jigsaw puzzles. How Mom taught me to recognize edges and fill in the picture from there. Hovering over the pieces, we recited poetry too. I remember how *the gingham dog and the calico cat side by side on the table sat.* They fought so hard, just like my older brother, Ben, and I—with our constant verbal sparring. In the end, the dog and cat ate each other up. I practically sang that part.

Mom would call out, "I have a little shadow that goes in and out with me."

I'd respond, "And what would be the use of him is more than I can see."

Sometimes we spoke the words together. "There once was a puffin, just the shape of a muffin, and he lived on an island in the bright blue sea!" These sounds, filling the space between us, were the closest we ever came to laughter.

My favorite by far was the tale of poor old Jonathan Bing, invited to visit the king. Those keeping watch turned Jonathan Bing away every time because he couldn't get his clothing quite right. First he forgot his hat. In the next verse, "Up by the palace, a soldier said, 'Hi! You can't see the King; you've forgotten your tie!' (He'd forgotten his tie!)" Finally, still in his jammies, Jonathan Bing went home and wrote a note: "If you please will excuse me, I won't come to tea. For home's the best place for all people like me."

My mom grew up believing those words.

Shortly after she turned fifteen, something happened that changed her life: the Russians sent up *Sputnik*, their first rocket ship. Mom's eyes lit up every time she told the tale. The dawn of the Space Race meant that in America, girls would learn math and science for the good of the nation. If she couldn't compete with her sisters in language, she could deal in symbols. That's how Mom became a math teacher. For a while, she even taught science, though it wasn't her expertise.

She'd given up teaching when she had Ben, widely known as a genius—as far as I could tell, since birth. Whatever he said, adults stopped to listen, nodding with rapt approval, to Mom's obvious pride. When I chimed in, their attention drifted away. If I persisted, they'd say I talked too much. Surely everything would change once I started kindergarten, when I could make friends my own age.

Mom and I shared this impulse to escape the shadow of older siblings. She overlooked the red claw marks on my brother's arms, my strongest defense against Ben's knowledge. He planned to work as a paleontologist, on the hunt for dinosaurs. I pictured him atop a pile of sand, scooping it into a pail from our sandbox. He, in turn, knew the names of every dinosaur species ever discovered by whom and where and when.

I exhausted what wisdom I had, trying to measure up. "Did you know flamingoes are pink because they eat shrimp?"

My deadly serious brother answered lightning quick. "We eat shrimp. Are we pink?" Since I was allergic to shrimp, yes, the welts would have that effect if I ate them. While I regrouped, Ben pressed forward. "Where did you read that? I don't think you did."

Flustered, I tried to stand my ground. "No, but . . . they do and I know it!"

Invariably I'd storm off, sputtering half-baked retorts. I didn't eat shrimp but he hated chocolate, which seemed important, if only I could line up my arguments. But the battle lines kept shifting. If I asked for peas at dinner, he insisted on broccoli—or worse yet, brussel sprouts.

I asked for a younger sister once, to help me level the playing field.

"No." Mom frowned. "When there are three, it's forever two against one."

"But I'll look out for her."

"Did you know Amy means beloved?" She reached out to smooth my hair and tuck it behind my ear. "You always wanted to be a mama duck when you grew up." She said this as if it made all the sense in the world. I need not go to tea with kings, just swim in whatever pond suited me best. Her subtext was perfectly clear.

When I went to kindergarten, I didn't know everyone would soon be watching me. On the first day, our teacher overheard me reading cutout letters taped to the wall. Mrs. W—a short lady with close-cropped hair—rushed over and grabbed my hand. Before I knew it, she'd silenced the others so they could hear me read. With unrestrained giddiness, I spoke the words aloud. "Welcome to kindergarten, boys and girls!" I had no idea how my gift would set me apart.

Banished during playtime to first grade for reading lessons, I learned secrets about those letters. Long *a* like *hay* and short *a* like *cat*. Silent *e* and schwa *e*. The rules all made beautiful sense. I also learned never to mention such things back in kindergarten. Once, when Mrs. W asked who could read the bulletin board, another girl raised her hand. She answered perfectly, word for word.

Mrs. W sighed. "Did Amy tell you what it said?"

"Yes."

The accusation startled me. "I didn't say anything!"

"How many of you heard Amy?" Several other hands went up. All eyes turned on me. My cheeks burned. I had read the words under my breath without meaning to. But I learned to pay better attention.

I still remember parent-teacher conferences that winter. Mom and I sat in little chairs at a worktable, wearing coats and drippy boots. I picked at traces of crayon while my teacher held up a purple ditto ink maze.

"Amy is so smart," Mrs. W said, "but she's so messy."

She placed the paper in front of us. Instead of drawing a single line inside the path, start to finish, I'd scrawled across the page in meandering colors. She pointed out my name, scribbled across the bottom. The room filled with quiet as the two women spoke. I stared at the posters until at last Mom and I trudged into the frigid Minnesota night.

At home, Mom sat me down with some coloring books. "You have to stay inside the lines. You can do it if you slow down." So I did. I learned a lot that year. Just not, perhaps, what the teacher intended.

One morning that spring, she made an announcement. "Today we'll have a visit from kids who aren't children." She peered around. "Who can tell me what they are? Amy, don't answer."

Of course I knew the answer, the same way I knew how to read: from watching *Sesame Street*.

The room erupted in chatter. Beside me, a girl named Jenny spun around. "Tell me!"

I was gone so much of the time, but I liked her best in my class. With our dark hair and pale skin, we even looked like each other. Still, I hesitated. "I'm not supposed to."

Her head bobbed up and down with excitement. "Is it brothers and sisters?"

"No."

Normally sweet, she now glared. "If you won't tell me, I won't be your friend."

I whispered, "Baby goats."

My friend's eyes widened. She nodded in recognition.

I was off reading when the goats came. I asked my friend about them when I returned.

"There were two of them." She giggled. "And they were so cute."

I twisted a lock of my hair. "But what were they like?"

"I dunno. A brother and a sister." After a few questions in the same vein, I quit trying. We both walked away frustrated.

&

By the last day of kindergarten, I knew how to blend in, but it was too late.

Mrs. W brought out our first day self-portraits and held mine aloft. "Look at Amy's picture," she crowed. "She drew herself with purple hair!" My classmates laughed.

Did I laugh too? Most likely I cringed. The eyes were also purple, the closest color I could find to brown before I knew it mattered. A familiar song from *Sesame Street* echoed in my brain as I looked at all the pictures: *One of these things is not like the others. Which one . . . doesn't belong?* Those kindergarten lessons would linger in a lifelong compulsion to make my handwriting pretty. And a deep-seated longing for friends more like me.

# 2

## Big Brother / Großer Bruder

Decades later, I picture myself at seven, floating out of a theater, the melodies of *Pete's Dragon* fresh in my mind. In the gray parking lot, Ben walks on one side and Mom on the other. She's happy to have started her new teaching job at the junior high. I'm happy too: Pete, a runaway orphan, found a home where nobody owned him, as his former captors claimed they did. Pete's new family simply loved him. The dragon that delivered Pete safely flew away, free.

I sighed. "That was the best movie I've ever seen."

Ben didn't miss a beat. "No it wasn't. *Star Wars* is the best movie you've ever seen."

Just like that, my spirits came crashing down. My first instinct was to rail against the arbitrary boundaries Ben liked to impose. But this was a losing proposition. Nobody ever took my side. Our dad, when he was present, would laugh and say I shouldn't have picked up Ben's rope. If I persisted, he'd bring out the big guns: "Young lady," he'd bellow, "you go to your room!"

When Dad wasn't around, Mom chose a different tack: she stopped taking us to movies.

She and I still watched *The Sound of Music* when it aired on TV that Easter. Mom hummed the familiar melodies while she corrected stacks of papers. And I learned: Nazis were bad rebels, singing nuns good. If all else fails, play along, then escape. Eventually the conflict ends. That was the appeal for me. The German language was incidental.

History would support my brother—*Star Wars* was empirically the superior film, whereas *Pete's Dragon* has proven . . . problematic. (Whoever thought people could own people?) I learned to retreat, still seething, when verdicts on such disagreements felt unfair. While Ben reveled in dock tag with neighbor boys down at the beach, I spun records alone in my room, dancing awkward circles and belting out show tunes. In that space, I imagined a life that felt . . . freer. I wanted to tell my side of the story, unfettered by outside opinions.

Four years later, Mom spent her days on the picket line during an extended teachers' strike. Dad was somewhere away on business. Ben played Dungeons and Dragons, holed up all afternoon in the basement with a crew of likeminded boys. Meanwhile, I stayed upstairs. I was eleven, poring over our hometown paper. Most every letter maligned the teachers, and school board members publicly mocked them. The errant words burned all through town, even at our Lutheran church.

One Wednesday evening, my choir director overheard me complaining about the hurtful comments. She spun around and blurted, "There's no money." Her mouth made the shape of an O when she realized whose kid I was. The director mumbled an apology and rushed away.

Except for religious instruction, I stayed at home, writing retorts I kept to myself. After six chilling weeks, the teacher's union settled for a humiliating loss. Classes resumed. The school board let go of all first-year teachers that spring as retribution. Some students staged walkouts one day in protest. At the elementary school, I sat outside against the brick school wall with a couple rebellious kids who went despite certain lunch detention. It wasn't a natural alliance, and it was chilly in the shade. After much deliberation, we went back inside.

Ben and I traded stories, helping Mom prepare dinner that evening.

"I have to write an apology letter," I said, chopping mushrooms at the counter. "But I'm not sorry. I'd do it again."

Ben smirked, nodding approval. "You should have seen the junior high. We flooded out of the building." He grated cheese into a bowl. "Hundreds of us walked to the high school."

I felt at once deflated and proud of my brother. "The teachers let you leave?"

"Are you kidding? They looked away from the doors so they wouldn't see us go."

Mom was notably silent, frying onions over the stove. Despite her weary air, she wore a slight grin. She had gone back to school in the evenings for her master's degree—and then they'd have to pay her more. She had tenure and couldn't be fired.

.⑦

Because she had surrendered so much in the strike, I couldn't ask Mom to give up her top seventh-grade math class. That was how she framed it. And she became my math teacher too. We went over the plan before-hand. "It's just for one year," she insisted, willing me to understand. "But you can't raise your hand often. You'll have to stay quiet."

"And what do I call you?"

She paused a moment. "How about you don't call me anything? That would be the easiest way." I nodded, her willing conspirator.

Mom brought me to school that first morning, sneaking me in the back door while the other kids waited, fresh off the bus and corralled in the front entry. Once they spilled into the halls, I slipped out of Mom's classroom. At the end of the day, I returned for my class, nervous but eager.

She didn't say hello. I sat in the seat indicated on the chart, off to the side, among my longtime classmates. Then she stood at the front, barely 5'2", and spoke in commanding tones. Reading her syllabus and then writing on the board, she hardly cracked a smile for forty minutes. I had seen my mother impassioned. Angry. Sad. I'd never seen her this cold, without even a telling nod. Even though she'd warned me about setting a tone, it threw me. When the bell rang, I left without saying goodbye.

As I boarded the bus, a girl leaned over the front seat and said, "Amy Hallberg, your mom's a bitch." I walked back several rows before sitting down, riding in stunned silence until the bus reached my stop.

When she returned home, Mom listened intently to my tale, frowning. "Let me see." Regardless of appearance, she was squarely in my camp. There were simply lines neither one of us would cross. A moment later, she flashed a fiery grin. "What's that girl's name? I believe from now on she's sitting up front in math."

Soon we all settled in. Mom and the other kids warmed to each other, while I managed to keep a low profile.

I learned to expect one question from kids who weren't in our class and barely knew me. I could see it in their faces before they opened their mouths: "Does your mom give you answers to tests?" They all seemed to know I earned straight As. Sometimes their parents made comments too.

"No," I responded each time, edgy but controlled. "I earn my own grades."

I had a harder time responding to my old friend Lisa, who took great delight in greeting Mom warmly each day. Once, sitting right ahead of me in English, she turned around. "Remember when you called her 'Mom'? You should've seen the look on her face."

"It wasn't that big of a deal," I said, shoulders tensing.

"Did you serve the detention yet?" Lisa continued.

"What detention?"

"When she wrote your name and then a check on the board. That was hilarious." She wore a huge grin, eyes fixed on me. "Oh, I'm not laughing at you. I'm laughing *with* you."

As the year wore on, I hatched a plan. Another film had caught my attention—the older girl across the street had taken me to see *Night Crossing* shortly after the strike.

In the darkness of the theater, I had learned about the Cold War. How, in the aftermath of World War II, the Soviet-controlled East German government booby-trapped its West German borders. They constructed a wall around West Berlin to stop a flood of East Germans from leaving. A secret police force, the Stasi, monitored every word and deed. They punished family members for any infractions.

But . . . two families managed to stitch a balloon in an attic. They floated over the border zone by dead of night. They landed, free, on the other side in West Germany. That bright patchwork of taffeta filling the screen, subversive in a world of gray, ignited a hunger in me that never abated.

In math classes once a week at the U of M, Ben had escaped all those watchful hometown eyes in Mom's classes.

And I decided to join him.

⟨✲⟩

Let's get something clear: those weekly university classes were never about my passion for math. Did I fool anyone besides myself? Case in point: my eighth-grade guidance counselor penned a congratulatory message soon after my acceptance, noting my exam score didn't qualify me. That's how I found out I got in as a girl. Mom confirmed it, and wisely told me to shake it off. I would hang on for two full years, though I was in over my head from the start.

But what did that brief detour make possible? Nothing less than two lifelong dreams fulfilled. For Mom, it meant she could apply—with my blessing this time—for an open position at the high school, moving up along with me. With my math requirement taken care of, she'd never be my teacher again, and I could study both Spanish and German. I'd start with one in ninth grade and add the other my sophomore year. I only had to decide which language to learn first.

⟨✲⟩

One Saturday evening shortly before registration, my brother's high school crew assembled as usual in our basement. Up in the kitchen, Mom handed me a tray of rye squares topped with corned beef, sauerkraut, and melted swiss. She was forever working these angles, trying to help me fit in.

The previous summer, she had dumped me in the middle of the lake, insisting I waterski. Mom had convinced herself that if I waterskied like

Ben, soon friends would also flock to me. Even though I screamed for dear life, having once nearly drowned attempting the feat, she refused to let me back in the boat until I got up. Bear in mind, voices carry on the water, and everyone could hear me.

Furious after several failed attempts, I grabbed on and told her to start the motor. And lifted up. I only went a hundred feet that time, but I mastered the trickier skills within weeks. Every day for a month, she pulled me behind that boat while I sang show tunes, voice drowned out in the rushing air. Mission accomplished, I'd let go of that rope for good at the end of the summer, still as friendless as ever.

Mingling with food was one of Mom's better ideas. "Take these sandwiches downstairs and wander around." She nodded and I sheepishly complied.

The rhythmic beat of "99 Luftballons," a German song popular on American radio, pulsed. It also had an English version, "99 Red Balloons," but as Ben had pointed out, the original German title didn't say "red." They were simply air balloons. Several lyrics had likewise changed in translation.

A tall, white-blond boy leaned against our stereo cabinet. When I offered him the tray, he said "Bit-te." It had to be German for "please." He took a sandwich, saying "Don-ke." Thank you. He spelled it when I asked: D-A-N-K-E.

"How do you say you're welcome?" I asked.

"*Bitte.*"

"The same as please?"

"*Bitte,*" he repeated. "*Bitte, bitte, bitte.*"

"*Bitte,*" I replied, half to him, half to myself. The same simple words could mean opposite things in German, and translations weren't what they seemed. But somehow German created a connection between disparate things—for example, my scrawny, professorial brother playing on the soccer team with all his popular friends. I wanted that kind of belonging.

$\mathcal{O}$

The German connection seemed to work. Early in my freshman year, I sat in sparsely populated bleachers with several other freshman girls I had started joining at games. Below us, the boys of the varsity soccer team scrambled across the field. On the track, cheerleaders wore blue-and-gold letter jackets over yellow sweaters and skirts. They jumped up and down, waving their pompoms. I knew a few from weekends in our basement.

Jill from German class pointed out two lanky West Germans who dominated the ball. "See the taller one?" she said. "That's Tilo. He's staying with my family for three months."

"Wait!" I spun around. This was a whole new angle. "What did you say?"

"Yeah," she said. "A whole group came to Minnesota. Thirty of them."

"Where are they from?" I asked.

"Baden-Württemberg." She was eager to share. "It's a state in West Germany. My brother will live with Tilo's family in the Black Forest. I'll probably go junior year."

I rubbed my chin. "So they'll miss school here?"

Jill tapped her fingertips together. "He'll go to school with Tilo."

"So they're at different schools in Minnesota."

"Yes." Jill sighed. "Two boys and a girl have partners here." She turned her attention back to the players.

I began weighing options. Only weeks earlier, Jill and her friend Shelly had walked to my house from school one evening and I'd asked them to move faster. Shelly had stopped in her tracks. "I've figured out why you're so anxious."

"I'm not anxious. It's just not safe with cars after dark."

"No," she said. "You're insecure. Your mother didn't pick you up when you cried as a baby. We learned about it in child development." As if the real truth weren't staring her in the face—in our hometown, everyone knew who I was: Amy Hallberg, teacher's kid, sister of a genius, fated to stand on the outside saving face.

I didn't see how I could miss three months of school. But the possibility energized me. I tried to picture my perfect partner, a West German sister chosen for me. I could learn German and get a fresh start.

By the time Tilo scored the winning goal, I had my heart set on this exchange. For the next two years, I bided my time, waiting for my turn to apply.

# 3

## German-American Friendship /
## Deutsch-amerikanische Freundschaft

I've often wondered what Eva first thought of me when she received my application for our exchange. In the picture, I wore my gold cheerleading skirt and sweater. I sent it hoping my new German sister would see a quintessential American cheerleader worthy of her devotion. I didn't want her to see the oversensitive girl who rode to school with her mother. No, I was no longer that girl. But enough people in my hometown remembered her that I had to set the stage carefully.

Granted, things had improved. For years, Mom had dropped me off alone at dance lessons and failed, timid auditions for local musicals. But her waterskiing experiment had served its purpose after all—bolstered by her example in earning that master's degree. I now understood that once I set my sights on a goal, I could power through and elevate my worth. My grade point average consistently ranked me first in my class. I appeared in plays and belonged to the speech team. Now I was the girl who had sat on the bench at varsity soccer games, bundled in a letter jacket earned for marching band. I chatted with my brother's friends and dutifully scored the game, never mind that I barely knew the rules.

Ben and I sat far down the bench from each other, reserving our comments for home. Me: "Did you really wear a Speedo for a Spanish class skit?" (He had, quite unabashedly.) Ben: "Sure you sold more Gummi Bears than anyone on the team. You were the only girl selling them. You're still going to fail physics someday." (So far, I had never failed science.) Nightly at my bedtime, he would blast the Doors on his stereo. The reverberating bass would echo through our common wall, sparking our heated exchanges. At school, we coexisted surprisingly well.

On game days, I had ridden the bus with my friend Teri, a cheerleader. And I had decided to join her—proving that girls like me could be cheerleaders. At the end of the season, the popular captain—a friend of my brother—coached me on jumps and the school song for winter cheerleading tryouts. With fierce determination, I had mastered my side splits within two weeks, nailed the audition, and made the wrestling cheer squad. It was hardly glamorous, and not a good match, but I was making inroads. If all went according to plan, I'd cheer for soccer with Teri the following year.

I wanted my potential German sister to see that version of me.

I hovered over Mom while she pored over my first essay draft. Finally, she looked up. "You're not describing yourself," she began gingerly. "You're describing who you'd like to be. You'd better mention how much school matters to you. And you're not comfortable in groups. Do you really want the most social girl as your partner?"

I railed at her suggestions, then spent the rest of the day at our basement computer, revising my words. In the end, I asked for an artistic girl who liked to act and read, not an athlete. Then I added two lines at the end: "I'm looking for a genuine sister. And she should be a good friend."

I sent off three copies and anxiously waited for my match. Luckily, I had an ace up my sleeve: our German teacher—an earthy blond woman who regularly interrupted class to process our feelings on current events—was on the selection committee. Frau K let us keep talking until everyone was heard. When Ronald Reagan made an ill-timed joke about dropping bombs on the Russians, or when we heard rumors of American flags being burned in Europe, or when the space shuttle Challenger blew up with a teacher on board, she was there for us. I trusted her to look out for me.

Finally, a packet arrived. Right there by the mailbox, I tore open the flap and pulled out papers describing the German girl chosen for me. I looked at her picture—she had cropped hair and a crooked smile, and she stared straight into the camera. I thought, *No, she looks nothing like me.* Then I flipped through the pages: Eva from Donaueschingen played tennis and basketball.

Mom came downstairs when I ran inside the house and slammed the door. I tossed the packet at her. "Eva and I have nothing in common." My voice trembled. "She's a sporty girl who doesn't even like soccer."

I retreated to my room. After a while, Mom knocked on the door. "Look again," she said. "Maybe it will turn out OK if Eva's not exactly like you. She's Lutheran, like us." Mom turned to the last page. "And look at her last sentence. She wrote that her partner should be a good friend. The same as you."

At school on Monday, Frau K met me at the classroom door. "What do you think? I chose Eva for you myself."

"Ae-va?"

"Aee-fah," Frau K corrected me. "You both said your partner should be a good friend. And I think you'll like Donaueschingen." She pronounced it Dough-now-*ESH*-ing-en. "*Ingen* means a town in the Black Forest. *Esch* means an ash tree. *Donau* means the Danube. That's where the river starts." I was letting that sink in when she added, "Jill's going to Donaueschingen too."

That was the sign that reassured me. That's why I said yes to Eva.

By that August, when we gathered at the Minneapolis airport, I laughed whenever I opened the mailbox to see Eva's jaunty script on a hand-colored envelope. Even though I knew my friendships had a way of fizzling out, I clung to the hope that this real person, writing letters, flying across the ocean, might somehow see me as I was, might truly become the sister who loved me despite the sensitive side I kept hidden. Or maybe because of it.

In the terminal, I stood beside my mother in my pale blue sundress, a ribbon tied to my wrist. Attached to the ribbon was a floating metallic balloon shaped like a mint ice cream cone. Bright pink letters taped to each side spelled out E-V-A. I'd spent all morning teaching Mom how to pronounce her name. All the other hosts held colorful signs.

Thirty-plus travelers flooded into the waiting area, searching our faces as they passed. All around us, people called out names in joyful recognition, embraced, rushed off. Finally the doors closed behind the last one. Mom and I stood alone. "What should we do?" My words felt pinched and small. I looked around, fighting back tears.

Then a gentle, high voice behind me asked, "Are you Amy?"

I turned to see a pensive girl with penetrating brown eyes. I exhaled.

She wore a bright pink crew-neck shirt and a ponytail. "I'm Eva," she said, her face relaxing into a smile. Eva hadn't seen my balloon, and I looked nothing like my picture. Further down the line, Jill had pointed me out.

Outside the airport, Mom snapped the first picture of us together. In it, we're standing next to a chain-link fence. Behind us, the plane that brought Eva still sits on the tarmac. I hold the balloon in my hands, ribbon still tied to my wrist, to keep it from batting in the wind. At the time, I noted with pride that the balloon matched Eva's outfit, down to her mint green jacket.

When we arrived home, Eva opened her suitcase and handed me a box. It contained a white watch with a leather band. Its rectangular face had no numbers, just gold hands and a single red heart in the upper right. Eva's father, who worked for a clock company, had the watch made just for me.

The following day, I was scheduled to work at the local amusement park, so Mom took Eva to register for classes. She planned to take Eva waterskiing afterward. When I returned, I found them in the kitchen. Eva hadn't gone waterskiing.

"Why should I?" she asked in a calm voice. "It didn't interest me." She ran her hand through her hair. Mom smiled sweetly, content to accept Eva's decision.

Eva was far more independent than I'd expected (which tells you how much I knew about Germans). She hadn't signed up for a single hour with me, not even our English and Spanish classes. Not even lunch. Definitely not German.

After their visit to the high school, she and Mom had sat at the table, talking about Eva's family during World War II. Mom would later tell me Eva's grandfather had been sent to prison for refusing to fly the Nazi flag, though his life had been spared because he was a doctor.

Eva broached the topic with me a different way. We went to tan on the dock for the last few hours of sunlight, lying out on towels, each with a novel in our own language. I asked to see hers, a silver paperback with stark black and red letters on its cover: Klaus Mann's *Mephisto*.

She watched me puzzle over the back cover. "He's the son of Thomas Mann. Do you know him?"

I shook my head and handed it back. "Never heard of him."

"You should read this. It's about an actor known for playing Mephistopheles in Goethe's *Faust*."

"And who's Goethe?"

"He wrote a famous book called *Faust*. Faust sold his soul to the devil, Mephisto, in exchange for all the knowledge in the world." And to continue performing this signature role during the Third Reich, the novel's main character, a thinly disguised real-life actor, likewise sold his soul to the Nazis, saying whatever they wanted to hear.

I grasped for a connection. "Have you ever watched *The Sound of Music*?" It occurred to me that maybe she hadn't. "About this singing Austrian family. They escaped the Nazis by crossing over the mountains into Switzerland."

"Austrians." Eva squinted and shook her head. "We should rent the movie *Amadeus*. You can learn about Mozart. He's Austrian too."

"After that, I'll show you *Hogan's Heroes*. It's a comedy about Americans in a German POW camp."

She smirked. "That sounds hilarious."

I picked up her bookmark from the dock, a postcard from a girl named Claudi that pictured the Donauquelle. The caption on the back proclaimed it the source of the Danube River in the Black Forest town of Donaueschingen. Eva had only lived there two years.

"Do you like it?" she said, her honeyed voice dripping with irony. "Don't you?"

She shrugged. "It's a silly little pool, magnificent and overdone. They say the river starts there, but nobody really knows where the Danube starts. It's kind of a joke for us."

"Ah, yes," I answered with a sniff. "This place is so much better."

✑

Home really was better with Eva, who never let herself be truly tamed. She was smart. And she teased like I imagined a real sister would. But it was a different kind of teasing than I knew. Her tone was playful, melodic, letting me in on her jokes.

Even Ben showed a degree of respect. As a rule, he ignored my friends to their faces and mocked them in private. I found him in the kitchen, eating breakfast with Eva. "Gullible," he was saying. "It means you believe anything."

"OK," she answered, even-keeled. "I've never heard of this word."

"Did you know *gullible* isn't in the dictionary?" He wore a straight face that I recognized well. The joke was classic Ben. If he were telling the truth, he'd be laughing. She studied him without saying a word and kept eating.

Eva and I both delighted when our family packed him off to college one weekend in early September. She wanted to see Chicago, and I would no longer have to compete with Ben for Eva's attention.

After he left, we established our own patterns. She would emerge each morning from behind the accordion wall that formed her make-shift bedroom, and we'd set out for school. She rode shotgun in my hulking red Ford Granada, circa 1974, inherited from Ben. I'd plastered a German flag with *D* for Deutschland across its bumper.

On free afternoons and every weekend, we lumbered around town, blasting the heater to combat the chill of rigid vinyl bench seats. We caught movies in the neighboring town and concerts in the Twin Cities. Dad mapped out routes across the Minnesota River. One week, while Mom stayed behind to teach, Dad drove us to Florida, with stops in Chicago and Disneyworld.

I could never predict what would impress Eva, who saved every ticket, along with postcards and wrappers. She couldn't stop talking about the stuffed pizza we shared with Ben on our way through Chicago, so full of toppings you could only eat it with a fork. She had equally strong—and surprising—objections. On our way to see the Norwegian rock band A-ha, she asked the first question that made me truly uncomfortable.

"Why is there an American flag in the front of your church?"

It was around twilight and we had just reached the freeway. "What's wrong with flags in church?" I said. I glanced at Eva's shadowed profile.

"We would never do that in Germany," she said. "We Germans aren't comfortable with flags. Our government forced us to fly a flag and salute. But Americans love their flag. You sing the national anthem at every event. This isn't something we Germans would do."

We drove on in silence while I turned her question over in my head. I lived in a German town on the rural side of the river. The Catholic and conservative Lutheran churches laid their cemeteries side by side, generations of families buried on that land. If a single Jewish person lived in our town, I wouldn't have known it. As relative newcomers, we chose the more liberal of two Lutheran churches. I had gotten as far as questioning communion bread variations and wine versus grape juice. Did you say "trespasses" or "debts" when you asked forgiveness in the Lord's Prayer?

Eva had touched on a blurring that felt not quite right. In elementary school, we'd pledged our allegiance to the American flag, which felt a little too prayerful. I had to remind myself not to say, "Amen." And as Eva had pointed out, in theory, we had separation of church and state. Did God really bless America above any other nation? Maybe we were treading closer to German sins than we cared to admit.

"No flags in church," I repeated.

"Absolutely not."

"But you would buy sauerkraut at amusement parks and pour ketchup on top."

"Of course," she said. "I'm a Kraut who loves Heinz ketchup."

"And German root beer at the State Fair?" We had already figured out that the drink was a relic of Prohibition, invented by German immigrants who owned breweries.

"No real German would drink that stuff," she said. "We think it tastes like toothpaste."

❧

Studying Eva up close, I picked up an inkling of what it meant to be a real German. The week the exchange group canoed in the Boundary Waters of Northern Minnesota, I tried out my fledgling accent. It was nighttime. Bundled against the cold, I stood under a tree, bantering with a guy from the actual Black Forest. (I could tell by his English.)

"Yes. I'm German," I insisted, using a CH sound for the G. My breath crystalized in the air and floated away.

"If you are German . . ." He paused to think. "Then what's the capital of Bavaria?"

"Munich," I bluffed in my pseudo accent, muted by the sound of lapping waves.

Perhaps he wanted to believe; he needed only ask me in his native language. In my third year of high school German, I couldn't have fooled him. A real German would've said the German name, *München*, knowing it meant "little monk" for the brewers of Oktoberfest beer. Eva had covered just the basics about Bavaria—*Bayern*—home of sauerkraut and lederhosen, those iconic short leather pants.

Had the German boy asked, I couldn't have sung the national anthem. Some guys played it on the out-of-tune lodge piano the next day, after they set the tables. Eva was there when it happened. She watched the boys sing with the same observant expression I'd seen her wear in Chicago. My father had taken a wrong turn, driving our minivan down a street where no other people were white, not even in the other cars. I realized at that moment I'd never been to a place where everyone else was black. It made me so uncomfortable I shrank below the windows, hoping they wouldn't see me. I couldn't begin to explain to Eva what that was about. I came from Minnesota, for God's sake. I wasn't exactly racist.

Unlike me, Eva knew how she felt about her country's unpleasant past. Walking through the woods following lunch, she told me about the forbidden first verse of the national anthem, never sung anymore, the one that began "Germany, Germany over everything, over everything in the world." Instead they sang the second verse, "Unity and Justice and Freedom for the German fatherland." Eva never sang along.

⌒

A few weeks before the Germans went home, our schedules changed, and we started eating lunch together with Jill's exchange sister, Susi.

Lisa and her best friend, Beth from our German class, joined us. Recently they'd invited Eva to a movie without me. Because she didn't want to hurt me, Eva turned them down. I couldn't control who sat at our table, but it drove me crazy that Eva connected with Lisa, the one friend I most wanted to leave behind. Meanwhile, Teri—the cheerleader by my side at every soccer game—resisted all my invitations to hang out with Eva on weekends, citing other plans.

Eva never seemed to have such problems with friends. She played tennis with Susi, who was so sweet whenever she joined us. They ate side by side, each holding a knife in the right hand, fork in the left. They stabbed their french fries and dipped them in ketchup.

"Strangers here ask us all the time how we are doing," Eva said. "They don't even wait for us to answer." Susi nodded. *Oberflächlich*, they called it—superficial.

"You eat french fries with a fork?" I asked.

They looked at each other and back at me. "It's much cleaner," Susi said. She wore her hair in a ponytail and a bright scarf wrapped around her neck, same as Eva. Eva had recently looked through a display of scarves at the mall, hoping to buy her mother an American present, only to find them all labeled *Made in West Germany*.

"You should hear the questions Americans ask us," Eva said. "Do we have washing machines? Do we take showers? Do we live in trees? We know everything about you. I bet you don't even know the name of our chancellor." We didn't. (His name was Kohl, German for "cabbage." Helmut Kohl.)

"That's so cute," Lisa said.

"'Cute,'" Susi said. "I hear that all the time. Everyone says my accent is cute."

Eva peeled her banana and began spooning bites into her mouth. "You eat bananas with a spoon?" I asked.

"Oh, yes," Susi said. "You know, if we are still eating, we will cross our silverware on the middle of the plate. If we are done, we'll lay our knife and fork together on the edge."

"But I'm an American," I teased. "When I go to Germany, I'll eat like an American." I held up a chicken nugget, Lisa grinning beside me, and for a moment, we were having fun. Susi snapped our picture.

Eva set her spoon across the tray, her eyes sparkling with a challenge. "You'll have to learn in Germany to keep your fingers out of your food."

"Even eating bananas with a spoon?"

"Especially bananas with a spoon."

Back home that evening, I made sure Eva understood the truth about Lisa and me.

"I get it," she said. "Lisa's not on your side. If someone isn't your friend, why pretend? But you'll have to take yourself less seriously in Germany. You're not going to be the best in our class. Your German is still very weak."

I argued with her, of course. Said I shouldn't have to take German with fifth graders plus two English classes. I thought I should sit in on all her classes. After all, Eva had done all right in my high school, and I was just as smart as she was. In the end, Mom sided with Eva. That temporarily ended the discussion, though I still disagreed.

We threw a party in the basement to send Eva and Susi off in style. Everyone came: kids from our German class, new friends I made through Eva, Jill, Lisa, and even Teri all came to say goodbye.

But nobody knew Eva like I did. Before she went to sleep on her last night, she filled two pages of my newly delivered yearbook from the previous year with references only we two would understand: our American adventures, her hopes and fears for my time in West Germany, and how she would never again eat ketchup without thinking of my funny comments.

By the time Eva crammed her souvenirs into her suitcase, I thought I had things all figured out.

*☞*

Once I set foot in Germany three months later, even the simple things felt hard.

Fresh off the plane, I took forty-one pictures tracing our path from Frankfurt to a stopover town on the Rhine. On the second day, I realized I'd forgotten to load any film. We were boarding the bus to Stuttgart, off to meet our host families, and I couldn't retrace my steps. I ran through the lost pictures in my head, mourning each one before I forgot them all.

Goodbye pretzel-shaped door handles at the bakery, and goodbye Mercedes bus grill. Gone were the photos of English graffiti scrawled on an underpass: "Amis go home." Pronounced Ah-Me, the same way Germans read *Amy* as spelled.

Loosely translated from German, Amis referred to foolish Americans. I had proven their point. All was not lost, though. I still had a thick journal with blank white pages to record everything that happened. I'd begun a list of words in a notebook I bought that first day. It had a line down the middle of each page: one side for German, the other for English. I'd polish my German and fit right in. Eva would guide me.

And true to form, she did.

My first evening in her home, following my very long nap, Eva held a partially peeled banana in one hand. She spooned fruit into her mouth while I ate the salami sandwich she'd made me.

"We'll walk to our school tonight." Eva licked her spoon clean.

"And what are we doing?" I finished my last bite.

"It's a surprise." Eva buttoned her jacket. "You'll see when we get there."

"You really eat your bananas with spoons? I honestly can't eat them like an American?"

Eva smiled gently and shook her head. "Amy. It would be rude."

"Then I guess I can't eat bananas."

She ushered me out the door and locked it behind us. Walking down the hill, I spotted black-and-white posters of two men and their guitars. "*Heute!*"—Today!—proclaimed neon-green bumper stickers plastered across the ads. A concert—a chance to start meeting friends. That was it!

Inside the school, we joined Eva's friends on the balcony overlooking the crowd. I strained to hear the banter, a mix of German and English. When the singer asked, "*Gibt es heute Amis hier?*"—Are there Americans here today?—I answered with a whoop.

"*Kaugummi! Kaugummi!*" came his lightning fast reply. The crowd laughed. I stood there, jaw agape.

Eva leaned over. "Chewing gum. American soldiers gave it out after the war." I made a mental note to add this to my journal.

At intermission, Thomas found us. He and his twin brother coached Eva's basketball club. He stood bouncing from leg to leg, his smile too eager. He'd be my coach too, because Eva planned to take me to practice twice a week. She greeted him with the pleasant equanimity I'd come to know in America. I already knew she found him irritatingly foolish.

"Come stand with me up front," he insisted.

Eva nodded. "It's okay. I'll find you afterward."

At the foot of the stage, Thomas held up a neon-green sticker. "*Heute*"—he pointed to the word—"I want to tell you that I have been waiting to meet you." The whole situation bordered on cheesy, what Eva would call "*Kitsch.*" Teenagers playing Kindergarten. But after two days of utter confusion, Thomas offered me what I needed.

He leaned forward. "Eva says you think we eat bananas with a spoon." His volume rose with the hum of the crowd. "It isn't true, you know." He chuckled. "She's playing a trick on you."

The realization struck me. Of course she was. I laughed, impressed she'd kept the joke going so long and relieved Thomas had rescued me.

I stood beside him, jubilant in the darkness. The crowd chanted "*Zugabe! Zugabe!*"—Encore! Encore!—whenever the music stopped. Eventually the singers ran out of songs. They sang "Tiptoe Through the Tulips" in falsetto while strumming ukuleles. I was elated.

Walking home, cars buzzing, I turned to Eva. "How long do you plan to eat bananas that way?"

"He told you?" She frowned. "I was having fun with you. Mom knew about it. Nice of Thomas to ruin that."

I felt the chill. I realized I actually might have enjoyed letting Eva's joke play out. Because honestly, I was lost in the language. Maybe I could use some good-natured humor.

# 4

## Field Trips / Schulausflüge

Adjusting to everyday life in West Germany often exhausted my brain. It seemed to me that beyond language issues, every little thing I encountered pointed to a deeper significance. For example, Eva's family lived in one half of a twin house on Geschwister-Scholl-Straße, named for members of the German resistance in World War II. I wanted to know more, of course, but I could barely manage the basics. Whenever I had downtime, I retreated to my ground-floor room to journal and sleep.

Every weekday morning, Eva's mother turned on the light to wake me. I hadn't eaten breakfast for years, but Mami set out delicate china plates at the dining room table. I forced myself to eat salami on buttered bread, plus two blood orange wedges. I gulped the hot peppermint tea. Then Mami piled her two children and me into her Volkswagen hatchback, and we raced off. She handed me my midmorning snack as I exited the car. Since German schools didn't have cafeterias, she picked us up at noon for lunch, during her break from the clinic.

In the kitchen, Mami would reheat boiled potatoes while Eva prepared salad. Her brother, Heiko, took the lanky dog out. I usually waited in the dining room rather than get in their way. Finally, Mami would settle her sturdy body onto her velvet and wood chair and ladle my plate with cucumbers in a sauce of fresh lemon juice and raw onions.

"*Du bist zu dünn*," she said. I understood this: You are too thin. Pull your chair up to the table and eat.

Mami would heap my plate with savory meat, tender from hours of cooking over the weekend. Then she bowed her head and prayed. After I took a few bites, she'd raise her eyebrows. "*Na, Amy, schmeckt es dir?*" Does it taste good to you?

My cheeks burned from forgetting yet again. I'd tell her it was delicious.

She would exhale, her face settling into a smile. "*Ja. Das freut mich. So ist es gut.*" Yes, that pleases me. That's good then.

After I cleared my china plate, Mami would spoon several scoops of chocolate pudding onto my plate, nodding knowingly. She'd tell her ruddy-cheeked son he was too thick and give me some of his as well, reminding me I was too thin.

By evening, when Papi returned, the usual time for our biggest American meals, I was finally hungry for the cold cuts we piled on bakery bread. I would gain ten pounds before I set foot in America again. Even then Mami would stash several boxes of pudding mix in my suitcase. She could barely speak English, but she never let me go hungry.

☙

It made sense that Mami looked worried when she helped me pack for our school trip through Greece. I was worried too. We would travel with Eva's former Greek teachers and classmates from nearby Freiburg. Eva couldn't go without me.

Mami came into my room and started to speak English. "You will this dress . . . need it. These pants, not."

I interrupted in my fractured German. "You don't need to speak English. I will listen." She was a child of the war. She'd never had the luxury of school trips or English classes. I couldn't bear to hear this proud woman, a doctor like her father before her, stammer.

Mami looked relieved. She pulled items from the pine wardrobe constructed just for me. "*Also, diese Jacke, dann. Das bringst du. Diese Jeans unbedingt nicht.*"—Bring this jacket. Absolutely not these jeans. She grabbed a few sundresses and laid them in the suitcase. "*Aber sei vorsichtig.*" Show foresight. Be careful not to draw attention or get yourself into trouble. In other words, don't make yourself a target for those who dislike Americans.

&

Mami prepared an amazing care package for our train trip. It kept me busy eating while the Germans talked and laughed. I never realized that when the treats were gone, I'd have to fend for myself.

Midmorning on our first day in Greece, outside the original Olympics site, the teachers gathered us in the grass. The man spoke in a stream of German, punctuated by drags on his cigarette. Eva sat enraptured. I picked at weeds near my feet.

After he finished, Eva offered a few words of English. "*Cook mao,*" she kept saying, pointing toward wildflowers strewn with chunks of stone. After a while I asked what that meant. Eva spelled it out. "G-U-C-K-M-A-L! It means 'look at that.'"

I soon figured out the stones were the whole point, the reason the bus had dropped us at what looked to me like nothing more than a rocky creek bed surrounded by olive trees.

"What are we doing?" I asked.

"We're having lunch," Eva said.

"I don't have any food."

"Right. You were supposed to buy some." She tore off a hunk of bread she'd bought in Olympus while I was staring at window signs. "Eat this."

Someone handed me an apple. I drank my half-bottle of Coke. Then I realized I needed a restroom. Suddenly I recalled the apple juice and coffee from breakfast, so I boarded the bus, closed my eyes, and went to sleep. I sensed my distended bladder bouncing even before I awoke. Uphill, then down, we wound through villages on one-lane roads. Water flowed everywhere, hugging the rock face, falling through air. Crosses dotted the roadside, commemorating fatal accidents.

I prayed for a singular goal: staying alive until I reached a toilet.

&

After that, I stopped leaving things to chance. I never departed any town in the morning without a loaf of bread, bought steaming from the oven, wrapped in a white paper bag with blue mythological images.

With each passing site Eva had to explain instead of enjoy, she grew more distant. In my journal, I recorded each perceived slight and eventual return of her affection, alongside the number of drachma I paid for what. Gum. A chocolate bar. A string of figs discarded when someone found wormholes. I gave up on describing temple ruins. Instead I bought picture postcards, each with captions wrapped around the edges—French and German, Greek and English. I compared the spellings of names.

In Athens, Eva arranged for two other girls to room with me. It was an infuriating relief.

The night before Easter on Crete, I reached my breaking point. We sat at one long table outside, waiting for our meal. Groups of three or four would share platters of roasted lamb and fries, or we could have salad. By then I'd been rationing money and starving for days. I started asking people near me if they planned to eat the lamb. No, they all said. Salad.

In faltering German, I tried to get someone's attention: "I need to sit by the lamb."

"Amy!" Eva sat farther down the table. "You'll get some!"

I resorted to English. "But I need to sit by the lamb."

"It doesn't matter," the girl beside me said, sympathetic.

With every empty reassurance, I grew more frantic. Finally, someone stood up. I stumbled to the open chair.

When I looked up again, twenty sets of eyes stared back at me. I felt overwhelmed and ashamed, but I ate. Later, I called Mom collect from a phone booth, distraught over the dinner. Luckily, by midnight a miracle had happened. During an Easter Eve vigil, I found grace in candlelit icons and incense. Orthodox priests in magnificent robes chanted their winding melodies. At midnight we filed outside for fireworks. Everyone hugged each other—and me.

We spent Easter Day on grassy bluffs by the sea. I pulled a paperback from my bag and leaned against a rock. From time to time I stared out at the horizon. The Germans played in the steel-gray water. They threw Frisbees. Whenever they checked on me, I looked into their eyes and smiled. But I read *Catch-22* all day, hundreds of pages long. I laughed aloud at jokes only I could understand, a tapestry of anecdotes about absurd rules someone had made up, but nobody knew who. The rituals never made sense, but everyone continued to follow them. And this made as much sense as any of the Greek myths I cobbled together from postcard captions.

I moved more freely through Greece after that. I let myself see what I saw.

Our final night in Greece, Eva and I shared a bungalow room. The other German teens joined us. We sat on the beds and passed cheap bottles of sweet Greek wine. We talked and laughed late into the night.

♋

Our travel through Greece marked a turning point for Eva and me. I learned to trust myself in the moment, knowing that if something confused me, Eva would explain later on—did a response indicate some secret German rule I'd disturbed? A joke I'd misunderstood? Or was it simply one person's way of being? Maybe even my own. "Yes, the coffee was too strong," she told me once, leaving a friend's house after brunch. "I didn't like it either. But try the mineral water. It's German. You have to learn to like it."

Because I knew Eva had my back, I felt safer taking risks. One afternoon, when she stayed late at school, I walked home alone. When I arrived at the twin house, a man stepped away from the doorstep. He said he needed to check the basement.

"I'm American." I slipped my key into the lock. "My German isn't good. I can't help you."

"You have to let me in," he said. He pushed past me through the front door. The dog leapt up, ferocious, but the man commanded him down. I followed the man down the stairs, where he looked at a meter and wrote down the number before striding out of the house.

Like me, the innocent-looking wire-haired terrier had a habit of being dramatic. Whenever he growled, Mami or Papi said *"Fui!"* and slipped him a morsel of food, stroking his muzzle softly. Now he was all riled up.

I figured I'd appease him, so I led him into the enclosed entryway and slipped the choke collar around his neck. He grabbed the leash in his mouth, a slight rumble in his throat. Startled, I dropped the leash and scooted into the house, shutting the glass inner door, trapping him. He barked, furious, jumping at the frosted pane, until Mami and Heiko came home and I told them what I'd done.

"You are never to let anyone in. Never. Do you hear me?" Mami scolded. "Do not do that again."

The waist-high dog led Heiko out the door. I apologized repeatedly.

"The dog is just playing when he grabs the leash," Eva said later. "But why would you let a stranger into the house?" I couldn't explain why, not even in English.

.✑

That day was the start of bigger troubles. One Friday night, Eva and I had plans to attend a party. First Mami needed to buy groceries before the stores closed for the weekend. I followed her toward the door, one foot still half in my tennis shoe, when the dog slipped past. I reached for his collar and called Eva's name.

The dog turned, bared his teeth in a deep growl, and lunged. He snatched the shoe, flinging it back and forth with a mighty shake. Then he dropped it and sank his teeth into my foot.

"Run, Amy!" Eva shouted. I raced to slam the door in the dog's face. I collapsed, shaking, onto the bed.

While Mami rushed to the store, Eva tended my wounds. A purple, tooth-shaped gouge glimmered on the top of my foot. It refused to bleed. A puncture on my sole bled profusely.

As soon as Mami returned, we drove to the hospital. The doctor and Mami stared at my immunizations record, conferring while I lay on the table. Eva stood by my side.

I clung to her arm. "What's wrong?"

"They're trying to figure out when you had your last tetanus shot."

"Right before I left America."

I started to shiver when the nurse returned with not one, but two syringes. I fixed my attention on Eva. "I already had my shot."

"You have to," she said. "The old one lapsed. You have to start over."

"Don't make me," I whined. Mami offered ice cream. I demanded to go to the party. Finally, I pushed up my sleeve.

"Not there," Eva said. "One in each hip."

I trembled as they pulled my pants down, as I begged Eva to stop them, as they injected me. Then they rolled me over, and I asked for a moment to catch my breath. While I was breathing, they shot me again. They sent me home with crutches. And Mami told me that Monday, the dog would be gone. In the meantime, we got to go to our party.

On Saturday morning, the doctor took the crutches away. He wrapped my foot in stretchy bandages covered by a blue plastic shower cap. While I hobbled down the hospital corridor, Eva interpreted for Mami. She said that in America, I would need three more shots for full immunity. Once home, I would discover that due to our different systems of vaccination, I had acquired plenty.

*✵*

Afterward, Mami and Papi decided to carry on with a weekend road trip they'd planned. The best thing for my foot, Mami insisted. A good walk. The dog rode up front in his usual spot at her feet. We drove to Schaffhausen, on the northern edge of Switzerland. There we saw the Rheinfall, the largest waterfall in Europe. I wore my new white Birkenstock sandal on my left foot, bouncing off the side of my bandaged right foot. With every step, I winced.

"Look out there." Mami pointed. "One hundred thousand liters of water per second pouring over the falls." A huge slab of limestone jutted from the middle. "Can you see on those rocks? That's a Swiss flag on top."

The white cross on a field of red fluttered furiously. We watched for a while. A boat full of tourists hovered near the base of the cliffs. We wandered into the gift shop, where Mami bought me a round black lacquer box dotted with Edelweiss flowers. For good measure, she bought me socks with Swiss flags around the ankles. Outside on the walkway, Eva's father waited with the dog, both subdued.

We drove to Zurich, a little farther south in Switzerland, where they bought me ice cream at a café. We sat, all four of us, looking over the waterfront, where ducks and sailboats bobbed gently in the calm waters. The dog occupied a spot under the far side of the table. I shrank back in my chair. Only when I'd developed my pictures in America would I look at photos from that day and realize the whole family shared the same downcast expression.

All that day, I limped along. I began stepping gingerly on my sole without resting my full weight on it. Back home, Mami and Papi handed me a couple dog treats, instructing me on how to make the dog sit and raise my finger to say "*Fui.*" Even before they told me, it was clear he was staying. I wouldn't be allowed alone in the house, and I would have to feed him plenty of treats.

I was terrified by even the tiniest of barking dogs for a long time after that. But I also understood they were doing their best to protect both of us, two beloved creatures acting on instinct.

⁊

My foot and my ego had long since healed when Mami and Papi made special plans the following month. Eva told me about the surprise while we walked home from school.

"We'll drive to Bavaria, to Munich. We'll stop at the *Zugspitze*. It's the tallest mountain in all of Germany. *Zug* means 'train,' and *Spitze* means 'top of the mountain.' We'll take a train to the top."

"Can we see Dachau while we're there?" The mountain would be nice, but like Greece, it had little meaning for me. And my exchange group already had a couple other trips planned. That *Konzentrationslager*—KZ for short—was the one important site visit not already in the works.

"I don't know," Eva said, quiet.

"I'd like to see a KZ before I go home." I knew modern German history was a sensitive subject. I'd never asked why my blouse, vaguely reminiscent of military insignia, had gone missing in the wash. What would I ask Mami if I had the words? What would she say if she knew how to tell me?

I'd gone looking and found her in the basement. Clothing hung from lines, left there to dry after Mami spun the excess water out in a cylinder. She was ironing the stiff clothing. Even socks and underwear. She looked so weary, I forgot about my shirt. Afterward, she'd brought me a chocolate bar, beaming so sweetly I covered my grin with both hands.

But Eva had told me many stories about World War II. She'd told me about the Geschwister Scholl, for whom our street was named.

They were a brother and a sister who had written anonymous flyers railing against the Nazis. When they were caught distributing papers in Munich, they were beheaded. Eva was so forthcoming about the Scholls' heroism that I thought we were on the same page in this regard. We were both raised believing in *Never Again*. You did that by telling the truth.

Back in America, my generation knew about those camps, had seen the photographs of skeletal people tucked away for hard labor until they wasted away or died in medical experiments or were gassed. And I knew Mami's family had actively resisted the Nazis. I wanted to understand what they'd been through.

I was also thinking of another white-haired lady back home. Cora was an elderly relative, Great-Grandfather Hallberg's second wife and widow. The day I arrived in West Germany, a letter from her was already waiting, written on special airmail paper. Cora spoke several languages and had traveled all over the world. She was also a devout Christian who actively believed the Holocaust had never occurred, an elaborate hoax perpetuated for God knows what reason. I'd never seen the magazines she kept on the subject—Mom and my grandma had told me about them. But this odd belief was in keeping with other things I heard Cora say. Like how I shouldn't drink Coca-Cola because it contained cocaine. Or how our last name used to be Hellberg until, thank Heavens, some minister's wife changed it for us to save Great-Grandpa from sin and damnation.

I wanted to understand this too, how well-intentioned people, German and American, could be so misguided. Maybe once I understood, I could explain it to Cora. I knew Mami needed no proof, but surely she would understand.

That evening, I heard her crying in the living room, Papi's low voice comforting her.

The next day, she came into my room and spoke in her simplest, slowest German. "We have to talk. Eva tells me you want to see a KZ. But I won't go there. We won't take you." She stood tall, unguarded. "You know my father died in the war. We also had to leave home. I lived in Königsberg on the North Sea. It used to be in Prussia. You know the meatballs I've served you, the *Königsberger Klops*? They come from there. Now it's part of Russia." Her eyes bored into me.

"Poland? Do you mean it's in Poland now?" I asked, my voice small.

"Not Poland. Russia. It's called Kaliningrad. I'm not allowed to return."

I didn't try to respond.

"My mother had four little children—one every year." She gestured with her hand to show the heights of their heads. "After the war, after the city was bombed, after it burned, my mother tore her clothing, put ash on her face so she would not look pretty. The Russian soldiers took German women, made them cook, made them clean, made them do other things." Mami paused to let me picture that, then continued. "After she was gone, we wandered in Germany, four young children with nowhere to go. The German people did the unthinkable. I lived that war. There were no winners." A shadow fell over her face. "My children learn about this. We do not hide it from them. Eva visited one of the camps with school where all those people suffered and died for no reason. My daughter brought her camera. She couldn't take even one picture."

"But Mami," I asked, emboldened to raise the one question that bothered me most. "If the war was so horrible, how did German people ever deny such things were happening?"

"Amy, they knew. Of course they knew. There were ashes in the air, the smell of death. But how can you admit such a thing is happening when you yourself do nothing to stop it? How can you live with yourself? They didn't want to know."

She stopped and took a cleansing breath. "I hope you will enjoy Munich. We will see many things there, will show you where Hitler stood, will show you the Hofbräuhaus where the polka bands play, will show you the tallest mountain in Germany. All this, I will show you. But," she said, eyes wide open, jaw set, "you mustn't ask me to take you to a KZ. I won't go."

And then she left me alone in my room.

.♔

In Bavaria, Mami and Papi showed me everything as promised, though it cost too much to ride to the top of the Zugspitze and come right back down. They made up for my disappointment by giving me an experience I could understand.

We stayed in Garmisch-Partenkirchen, home of a US army base. Everyone spoke English, so much that Mami couldn't order in German at the McDonald's where we grabbed dinner. Afterward, Eva and I rushed off to the theater to see a new American movie, also in English. It was a silly farce with mindless theme songs that stuck in my brain. One was a series of primal wails, a driving rhythm, a catchy chant: *Mmmm bam bam chicka chickachickahhh. Beautiful, more beautiful.* Eva and I enjoyed the movie so much that the next night, after our tour of Munich, we talked her parents into letting us return for an encore, complete with a repeat tub of salted—not sugared—butter popcorn.

I got in trouble from Papi on the car ride home for knitting my new sweater, not looking enough at the scenery, too afraid to mess up the stitches. Then I dozed off. When we stopped at a rest stop for lunch, Mami handed me a whole tomato, a big chunk of cucumber, and a cold pork chop wrapped in tinfoil. She chased me around the parking lot to wake me up for the rest of the ride.

I knew Eva's parents often thought I wasn't paying attention. In truth, when it really mattered, I was listening closely.

# 5

## West and East Berlin /
## West Berlin und Berlin, Hauptstadt der DDR

Whatever else I didn't know, I knew about the Berlin Wall. It represented the sorrows of a divided nation, the center of a wider schism between East and West. We American teens understood that significance when we went to Berlin on our own.

By 1987, the trip to West Berlin was routine. A train would ferry us across the East German countryside, making one stop midway. Stoic East German guards would pass through, check our passports and tourist visas, then exit the train.

By that point, Jill and I had spent too much time together. After we boarded the train, she went off to find other people we knew. I found a seat beside Nikki, a free-spirited girl we knew from our time canoeing in the Boundary Waters.

Now, rolling across East Germany, our group spent the whole time migrating between compartments. We compared the contents of care packages and the states of our German fluency. My peers showed off stolen rolls of toilet paper stamped with the letters DB for Deutsche Bundesbahn—the name of the West German train service.

When our train pulled into the Zoologischer Garten station in the center of West Berlin, our hosts for the week claimed us. I waved good-bye and set off behind my temporary family: a woman in her forties, her twelve-year-old son, and her fourteen-year-old daughter, all with short blond hair and pixie faces. They guided me into the city, then across a bustling intersection to a bus stop sign. There they handed me a pass, good for any public transportation. They offered running instructions on how I would backtrack to the Zoologischer Garten from their apartment. I'd have to return there on my own. In the morning, our group would meet up nearby.

We showed up bright and early at the auditorium near the Zoologischer Garten. In polished English, two speakers told us about life in East Germany. "They read all your mail," said the woman. "And they check any packages you send. You can't be sure it will get there. I once sent my friend a sweater and a lipstick. She wrote back, thanking me for the lipstick." I snickered along with my peers.

The man stood tall behind the microphone. "Our organization is making plans for the time when East and West Germany reunite. When the wall comes down."

I exchanged glances with Nikki and shook my head. Surely the wall that we had so far only glimpsed while entering the city—155 kilometers of concrete built and reinforced over four decades, protected by dogs, armed guards in watchtowers, buried mines, and entrenched secrecy—would never fall.

Before we left, the speakers warned us to pay close attention to historical context. Tour guides would show us around West Berlin for several days. We would see that wall up close, along with other iconic sites.

At the end of the week, we would spend a day in East Berlin on our own. And we would need to be careful.

Our tour bus dropped us several blocks from the Reichstag, a cavernous museum once home to the German government. To get there, we filed along the western side of the wall. There was so much to absorb. Layers of paint coated the surface. Words of protest mingled with poems. Glued-on mirrors reflected light as if it were shining through from the other side. Maybe through bullet holes. Paper mâché faces projected from the wall as if to evoke the spirits of those who still longed to pass through. And those who had died trying.

Profanity and prayer coexisted on those concrete slabs. We stopped to snap pictures and tried to keep up.

✍

At the end of our long first day, the tour bus dropped us off for a quick stop at the Potsdamer Platz. Center of Berlin's glory days, it had become a wasteland of souvenir carts. Nikki and I raced between stands laden with black, red, and gold memorabilia. When we returned to the tour buses, ours was gone.

We ran alongside the remaining buses, hoping against hope. At last, we stared at each other, stunned and breathless.

"Did they really leave?" Nikki asked.

"Even Jill?" I felt my cheeks burn. "How could she not notice we were gone?"

Nikki scanned the area. "How will we find the subway?"

I pointed to a road. "I guess we start walking."

We walked through empty streets. We wandered past uniform brick buildings, far from helpful landmarks. I muttered random comments about the idiots on the bus.

A few blocks away, we saw a girl on a bicycle, maybe around ten. We ran up to her and babbled in German. "Know you—subway, where it is the subway? Station?" She stared until we went away.

We continued for several more blocks before we spied a subway sign. Nikki and I raced down the stairs to the platform. Breathless, we hopped onto the next train. We pieced together what we knew of the city from a subway map.

"Look." She pointed to a dot. "Zoologischer Garten."

"Maybe we can make it back in time to meet the bus."

Sure enough, we reached the spot where we'd started just as the bus pulled up.

"Oh, yeah," said Jill when she found us waiting outside. "I realized after we left that you didn't make it." She walked off. A few guys posed in front of a statue, each holding cases of beer. The pressure built in my forehead.

I wanted to confront Jill, maybe some others, but Nikki stopped me. "Don't make a big deal. We'll only isolate ourselves more." I let it drop.

The next day, we boarded a bus and drove to the Haus am Checkpoint Charlie, a museum at the border crossing between the Soviet Zone that became East Berlin and the American Zone that formed part of West Berlin. I lingered at every display: a low-lying convertible used more than once to drive under the gate before they reinforced Checkpoint Charlie, a harness used to send a child out a window on a zip line before they bricked up the windows facing the Berlin Wall, the actual balloon depicted in the movie *Night Crossing*, which had caught my attention years earlier. I bought a book of photos so I would never forget the guards jumping over barbed wire and people tunneling out.

Meanwhile, much of our group left the museum to go exploring. On the bus afterward, a whole section sported hats with transparent green visors and spinning propellers, flaunting their indifference. I couldn't decide what Jill was thinking. She sat among them without a visor. That evening on a river cruise, I watched one guy down several bottles of beer in succession, cheered on by the others. Jill was still with them.

The following morning, she joined Nikki and me on the bus. "They only care about alcohol," she announced as we departed for a round of World War II memorials.

♫

As it turned out, I only cared about history. Specifically, the freedom fighters pictured at an execution site.

That's where I first saw Hans and Sophie Scholl. I couldn't get enough of their story. They were beheaded in Munich in 1943. There were pictures of their friends and a sample of their words:

*We will not be silent.*

*We are your bad conscience.*

*The White Rose will not leave you in peace!*

*Die Weiße Rose* composed six leaflets. *Awaken,* they said. *Stand up.*

They quoted Goethe. They quoted the Bible. They smuggled copies of those leaflets all over Southern Germany. They filled suitcases with contraband papers and crossed the country in trains. Hans and Sophie were captured at their own university when a custodian caught them tossing leaflets over the railing of a lecture hall. The Nazis put them to death four days later, but the Allies spread their message, dropping that sixth leaflet from planes. They were only in their twenties, students like us, but they did all that. Forty-four years after their execution, they could've had families. They should've still been alive.

"The Scholls were captured by a custodian," I said, sitting in the office cafeteria where our chaperones had delivered us for lunch.

Nikki and Jill exchanged glances. Suddenly one and then the other of them slipped their metal spoons into their bags. They took surreptitious glances around the room. I didn't stop them, but I felt uneasy.

"We should grab a spoon everywhere we eat." Jill said when we reached the stairwell. "We'll see how many we have at the end of the week."

"Definitely," Nikki said. She had a wicked glint in her eye.

Jill put her hand on Nikki's shoulder when we reached the ground floor. "Let's ditch this afternoon's tour."

Nikki looked at me. "Come on."

We wandered through the city taking pictures. We wore paper crowns from Burger King and posed beside modern sculptures. We took lighthearted snapshots at a damaged church that commemorated Berlin's near destruction. Nikki jaywalked across a busy street. A West Berlin police officer tried to make her pay a fine—she laughed it off.

The more serious the venues, the more German required, the sillier my companions grew. "Then let us revel in our foolishness," Nikki and Jill and the rest seemed to say.

I played along. But part of me wanted to dig deeper. To know why the Scholls rebelled, and how they found the courage. More and more, I was watching Jill and Nikki from the outside.

*❧*

The following day, we finally took the train into East Berlin, a short ride to a station across the border. There, we waited in a long line at customs to pay our entrance fee of five Deutschmarks and make mandatory exchanges: twenty-five Deutschmarks for twenty-five East German Marks.

That's when the bright idea hit me. "Let's take a picture of all these people waiting to get into East Berlin!" I held up my camera and snapped a shot of the packed room.

When Jill raised her camera above the crowd right afterward, two guards appeared, grabbed her, and disappeared with her behind a door. My temples throbbed as Nikki and I stood staring at each other.

"What are they going to do to her?" I whispered. "They'll let her go, right?"

"They won't hurt her. She's an American." Nikki raised her eyebrows. "But how will we find her?"

It seemed like forever, waiting in that packed room, trudging forward in line, finally facing an emotionless guard behind a window, giving just the facts he requested as he studied my passport picture, took my money from the West, and handed me his money from the East.

Jill waited on the other side, unharmed but distinctly chillier in spirit when we emerged. "They asked me questions I couldn't understand," she announced. "When they realized I was clueless, they took my film." She glared at me. "They saw your flash. I didn't use one."

I apologized profusely, but it didn't change what had happened. That's when the tension took full effect.

It turned out we couldn't take pictures of bridges and train stations. But we could take pictures of anything we liked along Unter den Linden, a majestic avenue of museums, theaters—even a university. I photo-graphed a block of carved stone that proclaimed eternal friendship with the Soviet Union.

We wandered through East Berlin, which several signs called "Berlin—Hauptstadt der DDR"—Capital of the German Democratic Republic. No reference to that "other" city just across the wall. Banners with the same black, red, and gold of the West German flag proclaimed forty glorious years of the Deutsche Demokratische Republik. Berlin looked in every way like a more solemn, grayer version of West Berlin, with boxier cars.

We searched half-empty shelves at a dimly lit market below the television tower at Alexanderplatz, looking for something to buy with money we would forfeit if we didn't spend it. In the end, I bought a bratwurst, a waxy chocolate bar, a Mozart album, and a mesh shop-ping bag with warped leather straps. I also brought home a raging headache.

.♔

Late in the afternoon, standing at a blockade, we stared at the famed Brandenburg Gate. Out in the No-Man's Land, only dogs and guards could reach it. My head pounded, my shoulders had knots, and my stomach was starting to swim.

"I have an idea," Jill said in a loud voice, facing Nikki. "We should go graffiti the wall when we get back to the West."

"You can't say that here!" I begged.

"Yeah, we should," Nikki replied, even louder. "We're going to paint the wall."

"No, really, you have to be careful!"

Nikki turned to ponder me. "I think you remind me of someone I know."

"Is that a good thing?" I asked, hesitant.

"I don't know." She and Jill were already walking back down Unter den Linden.

After we cleared customs and found our train waiting at the platform, the two of them ran ahead to another car, leaving me to find my own way back. I didn't care. I wanted to return to the West. I wanted relief for my head and stomach. After that morning's scare, I'd dropped my remaining coins, ninety-five East German pfennigs, in the street. But I met a new American girl on that train, another redhead, who gave me one of her coins, smuggled through customs inside her bra.

Back at the apartment of my West Berlin host family, I told the father about my day. He opened a drawer and pulled out a full set of coins he'd collected. "It's worthless over here," he said, "but they protect it like it's top secret."

"I don't get it," I said. "Why do the East German guards keep following orders? Why don't they conspire to escape if so many East Germans want to leave?"

"They pair unlikely teams, partners that don't fit well together." He handed me the money. "That way, the guards don't trust each other. If they want to rebel, they keep it to themselves."

It made perfect sense.

# 6

# Revisionist History / Geschichtsrevisionismus

On June 12, 1987, Ronald Reagan stood at the Brandenburg Gate and spoke the words that sealed his legacy: "Mr. Gorbachev, tear down this wall."

Reagan spoke directly to the Secretary General of the Soviet Union, America's sworn enemy, but we recognized his intended audience. Most Americans wouldn't know Erich Honecker, who came to power in East Germany shortly before Watergate. We all knew Mikhail Gorbachev, with his port-wine-stained forehead. He was the architect of Soviet Glasnost *and* Perestroika—Openness and Restructuring.

Watching President Reagan on television, Eva and I exchanged glances, noting the improvement on President John F. Kennedy's soundbite from '61: "*Ich bin ein Berliner.*" It was that fateful word "*ein*" that flawed the speech. According to popular translation, instead of naming himself a citizen of Berlin, John F. Kennedy called himself a "jellyroll." At least as his critics spun it.

Across the ocean from America, I was gaining a new perspective on my native land. Sure, we were free, but what did that mean when I felt so alone there? Despite my struggles connecting with fellow

Americans, from where I sat, I knew I wasn't alone in my disconnect. Lisa and her best friend had both sent numerous letters detailing two sides of a sinking relationship. From other classmates I heard long tales of prom drama. The letters from home made me grateful I wasn't there. My own best cheerleading friend never sent a single letter. And Jill was anxious about her old friendships as well. In that shifting landscape, what exactly was I going home to for senior year?

When I left Eva's family curbside in Stuttgart to board a bus bound for Frankfurt International Airport, other Americans in my group couldn't say goodbye soon enough. Looking out the window at a German waving an American flag, one of the guys said, "That was my partner."

As for me, I waved until Eva and her family disappeared. I cried all the way to the airport until my eyes went fuzzy from tears, the first of many I would cry over my return home. In the Minneapolis terminal, I saw Mom and burst into tears once again as we rushed to embrace. But despite the tears, I had changed in Germany. I no longer caved for people who didn't like me. I had made my own way back from the Berlin Wall. Twice. Mom noticed how much more relaxed I had become. Dad gave me more leeway. Even Ben, home from college for the summer, treated me with a newfound respect. He had hung a banner out front of the house, written in exacting letters: "*Willkommen zu Hause*, Amy!"— welcome home. The first time he questioned something I said, I sweetly offered him chocolate. He laughed and backed down.

This was the new Amy Hallberg. People would have to get used to that.

When I was named valedictorian at the end of senior year, a little-read local newspaper printed my speech and an interview. My graduation portrait in black and white headlined them: Amy as a pouty glamour girl.

At the open house party Mom threw, a neighbor, the willowy Mrs. S, sought me out. "I read your article in the paper." She leaned in. "And I have a bone to pick. You said it took one year to learn Spanish."

"That's not what I said."

"That's what they printed. I'm a Spanish teacher, you know, and I would have to disagree."

I looked around for an escape. "No, I said it took years."

"Well then, you've been misquoted. You should write the paper a letter. Ask them to make a retraction." She nodded. "If that's not what you said."

But I had said so, sitting in almost that same living room spot. In an hour-long chat, I volunteered my experience as an exchange student, the one thing that distinguished me from Ben, himself a former valedictorian. I told her how I'd faithfully followed him into math at the U of M, freeing up room in my schedule for both German and Spanish. I talked about the plays I'd starred in senior year after I returned from Europe.

When the reporter asked me to describe my fluency, I'd paraphrased a quote someone told me in Germany. "It takes a certain amount of time, I'm not sure how long, to learn Spanish. And it takes a lifetime to learn English. But it takes two lifetimes to learn German."

"How long do you think?" said the lady with mousy brown hair and round plastic glasses, strikingly similar to Mrs. S as she scribbled words into her notebook. "What would you say it takes for Spanish?"

"Uh, I don't know."

She peered at me, sweet but intent. "Do you think it takes maybe five years? Maybe a year?"

"Sure." I didn't think she'd use the quote. I'd said so many other, better things.

I didn't tell the reporter or Mrs. S that I'd dropped out of Spanish earlier that year. I'd fallen behind from going to Germany, and I hadn't bothered to review what I'd missed. Third-year Spanish almost cost me the one thing that mattered most: the title of valedictorian.

On June 10, 1988, nearly a year to the day from President Reagan's speech, I stood before my classmates and their families in the stadium outside the high school and offered my valedictory speech.

"I never felt so small in my life as I did when the Berlin Wall loomed before me. Too often, though, we impose our own walls on our lives: when we doubt ourselves, when we make excuses instead of facing reality, when we tell ourselves something is impossible.

"Thousands of people have risked their lives, and even died, to escape the confines of the Berlin Wall and become free. Last summer, thousands of young people in East Berlin stormed the wall, shouting, '*Die Mauer muß weg!*'—the wall must go. That took courage, but it takes as much courage for us to see the walls in our own lives and say, 'The wall must go.' What if other people laugh at us? What if we fail?

"East Germans have to live with a wall. We do not. We have the freedom to believe in ourselves enough to follow our dreams and make them come true. We should never be afraid to tear down a wall, no matter how small and powerless we feel when it looms up larger than life before us.

"The wall must go."

# 7

## When the Wall Fell / Mauerfall

When I graduated first in my class from high school, telling everyone that I was going to be an author, nobody was prouder than my big brother, Ben. To celebrate our shared title of valedictorian, he bought me an English dictionary, a thesaurus, and a vibrant woven friendship bracelet when he took me to see the Grateful Dead.

Wandering the parking lot before the doors opened, he navigated me past various vendors hawking their incense and chimes. After we picked out the bracelet, I bought myself a tie-dye T-shirt with rainbow-colored peace signs on its front and back. The sun shone in the clear sky, the air was the perfect blend of breezy warmth, and we were making our way through the crowd when a bearded man walked past and muttered into my ear, "Mush-rooms!"

We continued on, and as it sank in, I started to laugh. "That guy just offered me drugs."

Ben flashed his enormous telltale grin. When he couldn't keep a straight face, it meant he was telling the truth. "People have been offering you drugs ever since we arrived."

I slugged his arm. "Why didn't you tell me?"

"I didn't want you to buy them."

I rolled my eyes. Ben knew me far better than that. As we sat in the darkness of the old hockey stadium, lighters sparking around us, he leaned over so I could hear him over the din. "Smell that? Like burnt cinnamon toast? That's pot. Don't smoke it."

And I sat in the darkness, winding sounds and scents washing over me, and let myself enjoy the warmth of my brother taking me under his wing. I'd earned his respect.

I was doing all right.

From early in my childhood, Mom told me that if I worked hard in school, I could attend prestigious Carleton College in rural Minnesota. She would find the money. Once I arrived, I realized that admission and tuition were the least of my challenges. The place was riddled with former high school valedictorians, and the learning curve was steep. After three months in Germany, I'd only placed into German Two.

Hanna, my Korean-American roommate from Chicago, had tested out of French. When I first showed Ben her picture, he'd made a prediction: "She's going to hate you." Shocked, I'd called him a racist. He didn't back down. "You'll see. We're from a very small town."

Indeed, my roommate and I would struggle to find common ground.

Hanna introduced me to ramen noodles, prepared in my hotpot. She demonstrated the proper use of chopsticks. "*Ah tteugeoun!*" she'd say as the steam rose against her hands. Hot!

One night, we sat on the floor eating bowls of fat noodles and broth. Above us, her giant Matisse collage hung on our slanted ceiling beside my towering Cologne Cathedral. She'd returned from her political science class with Paul Wellstone, a well-known liberal professor who espoused a kind of social welfare politics.

"Sometimes I wonder if you think before you open your mouth. That's all I'm saying," she said.

"So you think people should get rewards for doing nothing?" I asked, slurping a mouthful of noodles.

Her dark eyes rested on mine. "How did you get here?"

"I earned my way. I studied and got good grades." The noodles slipped from my chopsticks and landed with a splash.

"Sure, but who's paying?" She stirred the broth with one stick.

"My parents. But I deserve to go here." My words came quickly now.

She shook her head. "What about people whose parents don't have money?"

"They can get jobs. Or scholarships."

"So smart people are somehow more deserving of an education."

"Well, yeah, I mean, no, but . . ." I twisted my ring. "My family's not rich."

"Right," she said, unflappable. "That's just it. You were born privileged, and you're ignorant." She got up and inserted a CD into her boom box. Metallic sounds filled the air. She turned back to me. "Did you ever think of studying in the library?" She swiped her fingers through her glossy hair. "You're always in the room."

I felt ashamed and annoyed. I quickly finished my broth, grabbed my book, and went out to sit in the lounge.

Sara, a sophomore from down the hall, came by just then. She'd also noticed my sheltered worldview, but she took another approach. "Hey, it's Yom Kippur! Come join me at Jewish House for break the fast."

"Breakfast?"

"*Break the fast,*" she repeated. "Where do you think that word comes from? We've been fasting all day."

⟡

It wasn't just social conventions that confounded me. A class called Foundations of Modern Europe nearly broke me. Despite my pages of notes and books filled with highlighting, I had no idea what the professor expected. He crossed out entire sections in my midterm booklet. "No!" he wrote beneath one question. "Your thesis, if you can call it that, is childish and idiotic." My cheeks burned.

After reading five hundred pages about Francis V of France, I couldn't even start my five-page paper. At a meeting in his office, the professor thrust his own copy of the assignment description at me, barking, "Why don't you read this very carefully and figure it out?" He then strode outside, leaving me among his overfull bookshelves. After five eternal minutes, smelling of fresh cigarette smoke, he sat back down and told me to pick one topic—just one.

"And at the start of a test," he continued, "take a few minutes to write your facts in the margins. Dates, places, names, details." His face softened. "Then you formulate answers."

I returned to the dorm in a panicky haze and called Mom. My friend Julie knocked on the door just as I hung up the phone. She had taken to proofing my work. "Did you figure out your thesis?"

"No." I snuffled. "I just talked to my mother. I told her I'm dropping the class."

"What the hell do you mean, 'you're dropping'?" she thundered. "You've got one week left, and you're writing that essay. Go talk to a tutor." I knew where it was: next door to the math help room, where I did all my calculus homework.

In the end, I pulled together five foolish pages and condensed my notes into a few sheets of memorized loose leaf. And I wrote straight through to the end. Around me, people stared at their test booklets or off into space, fingers on their foreheads. I could feel the tension in the air, and I kept writing. Midway through the final, one person stood up in the lecture hall. Others rose and began flooding out the door.

Lucky me, I earned my first C+. My GPA would suffer. But I passed—childish thesis, asinine assumptions, and all. I was never so proud of a grade in my life.

While I struggled through my first year of college, Eva and her friends completed their thirteenth year of Gymnasium. Despite its sporty name, *Gymnasium* meant a serious high school. Only Gymnasium students completed the Abitur, the test that determined their university options, including fields they could study. Not all Germans attended high school until nineteen, of course. At the Hauptschule, the most basic German high schools, students graduated after ninth grade. Realschule fell in between. But German students were tracked at fifth grade. Eva's friends all attended Gymnasium.

Presumably they were my friends too, the ones I wanted to see before they dispersed, so I found a cheap plane ticket over the summer after my freshman year. Only one problem: in the two years since our exchange, Eva had already made an entirely different set of friends.

On the evening I arrived, I sat at one of many wooden tables inside a giant beer tent. Eva, her new-to-me boyfriend, and various new faces crowded beside me. Under the dazzling white ceiling, the amplified, jumbled voices, snippets of disjointed words, and percussive din of polka music overwhelmed my senses. Then I looked up and realized Eva had left. I was alone with a table of unfamiliar German teens and, with one year of college German behind me, far from fluent.

I stared at their mouths when they spoke. I looked up at the stage and the band, the brass and accordion playing in 3/4 rhythm, drowning out German words that flowed too rapidly for me to grasp, even in a quiet room.

That's when I picked up the saltshaker, then set it down ever so slightly to the right. I nudged it a little farther. Now the pepper, just a smidge, as if choreographing a dance. Beside me, a tall, dark guy with an Italian name glanced at the shakers, then me. His eyes began to crinkle, hinting at recognition. Finally, he cracked a smile.

By the time Eva and the boyfriend returned, I'd made myself a full participant in conversation I could barely decipher. I hadn't been able to do that in the one English class I took for my original college major. When the music finally stopped and we shuffled out into the grassy darkness, the silence was deafening. I felt the blood stir in my veins. That may have been the moment when I had an inkling of my true calling as a German major.

I stayed with Eva's family for a month that time. In the two years since our exchange, they had built a new, larger home on the edge of town. Instead of sleeping in their office, I had my own room in the basement, and as before, they kept me well fed. After my year of college, Germany with Eva and her friends felt easy. I knew I couldn't live in her basement forever, but I'd enjoy myself while I could.

At a street festival on the edge of the Black Forest, I danced the familiar polka steps and sang the folk songs I'd learned in high school, while my German peers groaned and shook their heads. "Look!" I gig-gled, pointing to a poster on the white wall of yet another beer tent—*Deutschkurs für ausländische Kinder*, said the bold black and fuchsia let-ters. "A German class for foreign children. That's the school for me."

∽

Eva refused to study German or English as her major, even though I repeatedly told her she should. She had a true gift. She still sent me German short stories and taught me fine points of grammar. Eventually she chose a more practical route, joining the waiting list for medical school. But that was a long shot, even for Eva. She settled for business school, her second choice. That's how she ended up at a three-month Chicago internship mere days after I flew back to Minnesota.

That summer, Ben shared a South Side apartment with Sondra, a woman he called "just a friend." The three of them piled into Ben's beat-up blue hatchback one Friday afternoon and drove straight through to Minnesota, arriving at our parents' house after I went to bed. I awoke to the sound of their voices and staggered down the dark hallway. In the bright kitchen I rushed forward, unfurling my arms. "Eeee-va!" I cried, embracing her.

"Hello?" said Ben, his tone sharp with irony. "You saw her two weeks ago in Germany. How about Ben? How about Ben's nice friend?"

Shaking my head and chuckling, I turned to hug my brother, then ex-tended my hand to his female companion. "I'm Amy," I said. "Welcome to our home." She'd visited our lake weeks earlier with a group of Ben's buddies. I'd spoken with her by phone while standing in Eva's front hallway. I'd liked Sondra from the start. Meeting her in person, I noted with satisfaction that she bore a striking resemblance to me. I knew she was born in South Africa. Her family had left because of Apartheid. And I liked that as well.

It was an excellent weekend, as if Eva, Ben, and I truly were siblings—finally evenly matched. Even Ben's just-a-friend Sondra felt like family. For years afterward, I would keep a framed photo of the four of us together beside that rickety car. I'm wearing my old tie-dye T-shirt. I'm clearly delighted.

.⌀

I was mulling over signing up for Spanish my sophomore year when Mom suggested Russian. She'd heard good things about the new professor, and—she said—it would pair well with German because of the Cold War. When I hesitated, because Russian would also be hard, Mom added the clincher: "Ben's taken Russian, you know." That sealed it. However . . .

Even as I danced in West German streets, ready to declare my German major, I remained entirely unaware of the people assembling in East Germany, their voices growing ever stronger.

I found out about their protests one gray November day when I sat down in my new dorm lounge. Strewn across the coffee table, the front page of the *Star Tribune* pictured an unbelievable image: people stood dancing atop the infamous wall, hacking it to bits. The Berlin Wall had fallen, the East German government lay in shambles, and just like that, forty-one years of a divided German nation had ended, with nothing left to do but sort out the details.

I stared into the hall at vivid murals I'd helped paint on our brick dorm walls a few weeks earlier. I tried to imagine a world without the Berlin Wall, whose murals had entranced me. I was witnessing the dawn of reunification along with the rest of the world. Just when I'd finally memorized the Cyrillic alphabet.

⌒

When the dust began to settle, Mom stopped by my dorm room on her way to a workshop. She delivered a pamphlet from her Lutheran church, along with a candle. They commemorated the miracle of the Nikolaikirche, a Leipzig Lutheran church far removed from Berlin. That's how I learned what had happened.

For years, people had met at the church every Monday to pray and gather courage. They spoke their political truths through poetry and music, led by a pastor oddly named Christian Führer. On October 7, 1989, Mikhail Gorbachev traveled from Russia to East Berlin to celebrate forty years of the German Democratic Republic, and he doomed the regime of the iron-fisted Erich Honecker with a famous kiss. Gorbi had already called off Soviet troops when the doors of the church swung open, and protesters spilled into the square in Leipzig two days later.

When news from Leipzig spread, people gathered on Mondays in other East German cities, crying, "*Wir sind das Volk!*"—We are the people. And all it took was the courage to tell the truth.

⌒

I wanted to experience this new Germany from a more grown-up perspective. A film course for my new major filled in some of the gaps on how we had arrived at this place.

During the opening scenes of the black-and-white *Triumph of the Will*, I sat in stunned silence. Hitler's plane flew in above the clouds. His Mercedes waited as he emerged from the open door. He rode past throngs in the streets, greeted with adulation: German women in dirndls and hats, blond children, all craning their necks for a glance at the Nazi Führer, seated tall in his open car, offering him salutes that were captured for all time. He got out and walked among them—a proud people stripped of their dignity following World War I.

The pageantry grew so tedious I nodded off. After the first hour and a half, I walked out, horrified at my complacency.

*Germany Pale Mother* hit closer to home the following week. A mother with her daughter wanders through large expanses of Germany. They navigate bombed-out cities and train stations and snow-covered forests. Her husband was never a Nazi. This was all she knew about him, and the only reason she married him, but they were happy in their finery. Ironically, as a non-party member, he was drafted first into Hitler's army. And so he's off fighting on the front lines.

The more the mom feels like crying, the more she sings and dances with her child, weaving too-real horrors into a fairy-tale narrative. When the father returns to sort through the rubble, a cold war continues at home. He lashes out at the child and controls the wife. In truth they don't know him or need him. His prospects are shot, and he feels betrayed. The mother lashes out too, when she doesn't withdraw.

Late one night, husband gone, the mother retreats into the bathroom, blows out the pilot light for the water heater, and prepares to die. The little girl stands at the door, pounding. "Mommy, come out!" she cries. "I am so alone. Please come out."

At last, the mother opens the door, but her eyes reveal the truth: she's already gone.

⁊

After seeing the film, I returned to my dorm room to call my mother, gasping out words while I sobbed. "This story could be my story," I finally managed.

I grew up admiring the jubilant wedding photos of my parents, first-generation college students who met at the U of M and married in my father's church soon after graduation. But those photos don't tell the full story. Dad often traveled for work, but he'd tried his darnedest to keep me in check, and we'd tangled. The words *young lady* still made me want to scream when Mom had raised us nearly single-handedly. She, Ben, and I had traveled the education system together. Sometimes we struggled to find our footing. Sometimes when it all got too heavy, especially during the hard times, Mom would melt down at dinnertime, losing her temper and yelling, then rushing off to her bedroom in tears. While Ben and I washed and dried dishes, voices barely a whisper, she would slip out the door and down to the lake. But she always returned. Mom was our most loyal ally. I couldn't bear the thought of her gone.

"It's not your story," she cooed, bringing me back to the present.

"Yes, because I was born at a different time in a different country." I finally exhaled. "There's no happy ending for people who lived through that war."

"It's okay," she said. "You're safe."

"I never realized what it was like."

"Then you're learning. Get some sleep."

I realized something else that night: the story was even closer to Mom's. She grew up on the poor side of town, the child of immigrant orphans who screamed at each other a lot. They were children raising children. "I was an unplanned third daughter, born to parents who never chose girls' names," Mom reminded me whenever she grew impatient. "Nine months after Pearl Harbor." That was my cue to back off.

My own past was littered with extended waits long after dance and music lessons had ended, the ones the other moms stayed to watch. When Mom's car pulled up to the curb, I rushed to open the door and never asked why she was late. Not even when I walked home from one end of my hometown to the other. I was eleven. That time, Mom barreled down the highway once she remembered. She picked me up a quarter mile from our house.

Mom clearly loved me and said so often. She bought thick books of crossword puzzles and told me I was the smartest girl from the time I was young. These days her entire salary paid my college tuition. She sold tickets to sporting events at school every evening, thrilled to fund the private voice lessons I'd started taking. She and Dad drove to campus for all my choir concerts, Friday evenings at the end of her school week, though she could barely stay awake in the darkened auditorium.

Scars from her youth made certain truths harder to face. Whenever I went away, Mom sent letters pouring out words she never said aloud. "There are painful patterns in our family," Mom wrote me at college after that late-night phone call. "I grew up in a toxic house. You're the one who can break that cycle."

# PART TWO

# Wiedervereinigung / Reunification

1990–2009

# 8

# Sound Shifts / Lautverschiebungen

As a German literature major I spent countless hours in the library, reading the literary canon from earliest times to modernity. In all honesty, the texts usually overwhelmed me. Sometimes it took an hour to read a few pages, and it took a few chapters before I caught on. I usually nodded off at some point. But I'd soon rouse myself and keep going.

And then one day, I settled into a library chair to read the English translation of Hermann Hesse's *Demian*. I expected another drowsy read—it had been released soon after World War I.

Its epigraph startled me wide awake. "I only wanted to try to live in accord with the promptings which came from my true self. Why was that so difficult?"

*Demian* recounted the story of a young man guided toward the secrets of life by a mysterious woman named Frau Eva. (Clearly Hesse had witnessed the depths of my soul.) And then he said this:

The bird fights its way out of the egg.

The egg is the world.

Who would be born must destroy a world.

The bird flies to God.

An expansive energy filled me. Only by abandoning an old life could I start fresh. Germans as a nation were doing that. I was doing that too. I devoured the book within hours and exited the library, blood pulsing. I found myself skipping across campus to the music hall, the autumn leaves more vibrant than ever before.

"As long as the dream is your fate, that is how long you must remain true to it," Hesse's Frau Eva said. The words felt exactly like an answered prayer.

*❧*

I once dreamed of marrying a college sweetheart, as my parents had done. A chance and otherwise unremarkable freshman-year romance changed that trajectory.

At Midwinter Ball, my newly beloved waltzed me around the ball-room, me in black velvet with rhinestones, he in the tuxedo he wore to perform with the college Chamber Singers. His dark hair shone, and his blue eyes sparkled as he gazed at me. It was the prom I never attended in high school.

"You are so incredible," he murmured, holding me against his chest. "So beautiful."

"I'm so lucky," I answered, blissful in his arms. So fortunate that a guy in my calculus class had set us up the previous week for an event tastefully called Screw Your Roommate. How delightful that my beloved's choir was rehearsing *Of Thee I Sing*, the same obscure Gershwin musical I'd starred in at high school the previous year, playing the role of all-American Mary. She wins the heart of the leading man—and presidential candidate—who chooses Mary and her corn muffins over a beauty contest winner who sings like a dream. In a convenient plot twist, Mary gets pregnant at the right moment. For good measure, she gives birth to twins.

Walking home under the stars, I saw a similar future unfolding with my brilliant man.

He took me to the music hall a few days later and led me to a practice room. He'd brought the sheet music so he could accompany me for the musical's love theme. As the first notes escaped my lips, disappointment flashed in his eyes, and his shoulders tensed. Suddenly self-conscious, I heard my voice, heavy and unwieldy. Walking back to my dorm, my chosen one informed me that the show's humor was incredibly outdated.

The following weekend, following a boozy Chamber Singers party to which I wasn't invited, he dumped me for a soprano. "You're so special," he said before we parted ways.

I was stunned. And pissed off. I nursed my bruised ego for weeks.

Then one day, defiance and my little-sister instincts kicked in: forget Prince Charming. If my former beloved could take voice lessons, so could I. Before I graduated, I would join those Chamber Singers myself.

Singing for fellow voice students onstage, I often forgot to breathe, gasping for words. Still, I persevered. It took almost two years to free up my voice enough to earn my spot, but I knew I was making progress with my German Lieder and show tunes. Once a couple music students peeked inside my practice room to see who possessed such a beautiful voice.

To claim my spot in the ensemble for junior year, I passed up an off-campus seminar in the newly reunified Berlin. Ironically, as a result I developed a passion for teaching German. Because I'd stayed on campus, my professors engaged me as a language assistant, training me to run grammar drill sessions and administer tests. To my great surprise, leading small groups of students in cautious German dialogue felt as enticing as singing on stage.

Slowly, I hatched a new plan: since I didn't want to teach high school like Mom, I would become a German professor, following Ben on the PhD track. To qualify, I needed to build German fluency. Visits to Eva wouldn't suffice—no way did I plan to repeat foolish past performances. Before my comprehensive exam, I also had that literary canon to finish reading. That's how I ended up at Middlebury German summer school prior to senior year, pledging to use only German under penalty of banishment from the verdant campus. And I delighted in keeping my word.

For seven weeks, I studied language structure under the watchful eye of Frau W, an exacting grammar maven. For the first time in America, I belonged to a sprawling group of friends. We went to film nights. A couple guys were publishing a German newspaper during their free time. On weekends, we rode the rolling countryside in open-top Jeeps. We met in the basement for a running game of hearts, played in the pidgin German of two California surfer dudes. I bantered with Tony, an Ivy League scholar who—when I stopped by in search of his roommate—pointed out the framed photo of his girlfriend on his desk. It was a summer of harmless flirtations and friendships, conducted in German.

In the afternoons, I attended a *Kabarett* workshop. A member of a former troupe in East Berlin had arrived on campus, wife and two children in tow, fresh from reunification. He taught us about subtext.

"*Kabarett* is about doing things for your own reasons, rather than following protocol," he said once. He looked at each of us in turn.

"Sometimes while following protocol."

As our show approached, our leader handed me some lyrics and a green feather boa. "Dance. Sing it loud and low. Work the room like Marlene Dietrich."

I had a feeling I could pull it off. My pattern with men was all about subtext. The less interest I showed, the more appealing they found me. When a man wouldn't hear no, I'd take a page from my childhood and pitch a fit. If I couldn't wriggle free, crying worked wonders. I'd perfected the role of siren temptress on Chicago's South Side. Under my brother's watchful eyes, his friends never touched me. I was prepared for *Kabarett*.

The night of the show, light flashed on me in the corner. "Let other women like the men they do." I intoned the German with a deep growl and stepped into the audience. "I have nothing against that."

I scanned the darkened faces, feathers trailing. "But as for me, I like one kind of man." I reached the school's director, a sturdy man, and ran my fingers over his silvery hair. "And he has always been there." I perched myself on his lap. "Always will be."

Now I rose up, belting the chorus. "Any man will do, so long as he has power." I took one final glance back. "Only he will be the victor."

At a reception after the show, I felt a hand on my shoulder. There stood my platinum blond grammar teacher, Frau W.

"Your performance was magical," she said. "And your article in the paper was impressive."

I blushed. I hadn't dared show it to Frau W.

There were no happy endings in German Film, I had claimed in "The Big Cry," featured prominently on page three of the *Sommerschule Kurier*. This came remarkably close.

"You remind me of my favorite aunt," I murmured.

Frau W smiled slightly as I tripped over my words. She raised her glass in my direction. German knowledge was glamour there. It was a heady, fantasy world, wondrous while it lasted. And—I hoped—a preview of grad school.

.♀

Pictures from a boozy gathering back at the dorm showed me draped across my willing Ivy League friend. He'd commented on how smart I was. I wore my jungle-green dress with cutout back. At some point, I led him back to my private room.

We only kissed. Still . . . that final evening, I didn't send him away from my twin bed in the sweltering concrete dorm. When I awoke still wrapped in his arms, a tiny fan buzzed in the open window. Daylight flooded the room.

"My mom and girlfriend will be here in a few hours," he said. "I need to pack."

"Do we have time for breakfast?" My parents wouldn't arrive for another day.

We threw on T-shirts and shorts. He peeked out the door. We stole down the deserted hallway and into the stairwell, slowing once we reached a playground at the edge of campus. On our way back from the bakery, we sat on two playground swings and pushed our toes against the ground.

"You had me confused last night," he said. "You were sitting on my lap while talking about your Harvard application."

My knees tingled. "Maybe we'll see each other again if they accept me."

"I can't see why they wouldn't." He paused. "Do you have a boyfriend back home?"

"If I did"—I popped the last bit of croissant into my open mouth—"I wouldn't be here with you."

"Ouch."

I licked almond paste off my fingers and shrugged.

We parted at the front door of the utilitarian dorm. Tony snuck up to say goodbye while his mom and girlfriend waited at the car. In my overheated, half-packed room, we stood motionless, holding each other for a long moment.

"Please keep in touch," he said.

⌒

Once I returned to my chilly Minnesota campus, I wrote Tony a letter apologizing for my behavior; I wasn't that kind of a girl. Things became real when he wrote back. He'd broken up with the girlfriend because of what I had said. It excited me when he called. Tony spoke German, of course, and he did go to Harvard. He was both insightful and logical. A photo he sent from that summer showed me radiant in his presence. And—as he noted—beautiful.

I wanted to believe Tony was the one. But when my witty Ivy League scholar showed up on the doorstep of the prosaic German House, where I lived, I couldn't fake my way out. Though I'd invited him, I felt cornered. I mostly hid in the library that frigid November weekend. I snuck off to coffee with girlfriends and played it cool when he found me, citing my comps exam.

One look at Tony in that harsh Minnesota light, wearing his bold Harvard sweatshirt, told me I loved the idea of him. I didn't actually know him. And I wasn't sure about Harvard. We shared one half-hearted weekend in my dorm room and a quixotic movie in Minneapolis.

When Tony was safely back in Boston, I wrote him an overblown email. I told him I'd made a mistake and asked him never to contact me. I don't remember exactly how many times he reached out, but I stood my ground with all kinds of twisted logic, all delivered in writing, refusing to let him convince me. He'd played all his cards right. I simply didn't trust myself enough to discuss it, for fear he would expose me as a fraud.

Harvard didn't accept me, and neither did Yale. But Harvard rejected Ben too, as an undergraduate—the only school ever, among prestigious programs that actively vied for him. After he graduated from Chicago, Ben moved on to Seattle. He'd discovered a passion for Physical Oceanography—meaning a focus on climate, not dolphins. Mom displayed Ben's senior honors thesis on the living-room piano music rack for months, something about particle waves. I cracked it open once and nearly drowned in the first sentence. I closed it again and set it down to admire its yellow-gold cover.

I received attractive offers from both his universities, each with a full year in Germany. Chicago was hard to say no to after my time there, connecting with Ben and Sondra. Riding shotgun to their favorite haunts. Eating at their favorite Thai restaurant, dousing the fire with sticky-sweet iced coffee and cream. Even waking up in their cockroach-ridden apartment after a party for Ben. My head was spinning and our parents were arriving that afternoon for graduation. He'd gotten me into a bar—visibly unsteady—by vouching for me as his older sister. At the time, I was nineteen. The guy behind the counter had winked and handed me an Anheuser-Busch bumper sticker that said, "Know when to say when."

When Sondra realized I couldn't sit up without vomiting in the morning, she lovingly stirred me a glass of cola until it was flat, saying it would settle my stomach. Their third roommate, a guy I barely knew, wandered in and addressed me in German. "You realize they're together, right? They're hiding the truth from your parents."

"I figured."

After graduation, Sondra moved to California and Ben drove to see her when he could. Try as I might, I couldn't picture myself living in Chicago without them. Over spring break, I flew out to visit Ben in Seattle and check out the campus.

I kept a list of reasons to say yes. The professor I met over coffee openly admired my writing. She said Yale had made a mistake. The well-stocked German section of the library looked out onto gorgeous green views. I couldn't figure out why I was leaning toward no.

Hanging out in Ben's apartment that evening—after washing our dishes in his galley kitchen—I'd convinced him to watch *The Sound of Music*, since nothing else was on, and he was actively listening, raising his eyebrows at some of the lines. "You know, this is actually funny."

"I told you!" I grinned and gently slapped his arm. "Remember when we didn't like each other?"

"We liked each other." He smiled. "Remember that game we used to play? You'd ask for peas or corn so I'd choose another vegetable, like asparagus?"

"I genuinely didn't like asparagus," I said. "And that game wasn't fun."

"Huh." He met my eyes, speechless for a moment. "I'm sorry. I always liked you."

Just then the phone rang. The professor had excellent news. Instead of a teaching assistantship, she was pleased to offer me a position as her research assistant. I felt honored and sad.

"Listen, Amy," Ben said when I got off the phone. "Choose the graduate program that's best for you. I'll make sure you have money to pay for it no matter what." His loving words meant everything.

Ben got me back to the airport so late the next morning that I barely caught my flight. I could have predicted it based on childhood patterns. But I couldn't fault my brother when the truth was crystal clear. He'd taken time to host me and driven me all over town—though on principle he biked everywhere possible, except to the grocery store, to drop off recycling, and to visit Sondra. Ben followed his passions as a climate scientist. I'd follow mine.

⌒

For the remainder of the year, I settled into Romantic poetry, passionately unpacked for us by a lovable, white-haired professor. Mornings and evenings I spent in that library, noting such distinctions as Goethe's *Sturm und Drang* versus Goethe's Classicism. Anytime I needed to stretch, I wandered in search of friends tucked away, equally grateful for study breaks. Late afternoons, they'd find me in the student union, flipping flashcards and drinking herbal tea.

One Saturday in May, I finished my five-hour comprehensive exam, then slapped my forehead and silently laughed, rereading my analysis of Goethe's "Welcome and Farewell": "The energy of the poem builds, moving faster, ever more passionate toward its climax, and then, having reached its peak—a release, a slowing, a pulling apart." I added a few sentences acknowledging my Freudian subtext and left it alone.

My instincts would earn me neither true love nor honors in my major. But the night before graduation, I had every reason to chicken dance, making merry in the street: Washington University in St. Louis had offered everything I could possibly want.

⟨❧⟩

Don't let anybody tell you German literature doesn't inspire passion.

A fellow Carleton grad who'd also ended up in St. Louis told me a disturbing story after we started hanging out, weeks after I moved to Missouri. He'd made a habit of arranging clandestine interludes with his college girlfriend in our former library, two floors below ground. They would spread out a blanket in the dim and dusty room where *Demian* resided with the German-to-English translations, because "nobody ever went down there."

I slugged him in the arm. "Nobody except me!" No wonder that room creeped me out.

At my new university, the whole library left me cold and lonely. So I stayed home. Living alone spooked me too. The walkup in my neighborhood was the first place I found with a chain and not a panic button inside its hollow door. I still couldn't shake the irrational fear that someday, they would find my expired body slumped over a notebook at the kitchen table Mom and I had recently picked out.

On hearing about my PhD program, most people I met would tip their eyes upward, mulling it over. Then they opened their mouths.

"*Sprechen Sie Deutsch?*"—Do you speak German? The question—the disconnect—made my stomach turn. Most everything did.

I distracted myself with a term paper, choosing the book for its friendly title: *Jenny*, by Fanny Lewald, available only as a photocopy in old-fashioned German typeset. Sprawled across my living-room futon, I deciphered the tale of a Jewish woman in the late 1800s. Jenny converts to Christianity to marry her beloved against her family's wishes, but she can't make herself fit social conventions. And so, she never marries.

Holed up in my bedroom, I composed thirty pages, turning them in a month and a half into the term. Around that time, my new cohort and I learned about Grimm's Law: how English, German, Swedish, and Dutch evolved from a common source.

"Indo-European?" I tapped my fingers against my notebook. "An ancient language that doesn't exist?"

"Traces in languages point to its existence in theory," said Gene, our resident linguist.

"Sound shifts," read Pati, who'd majored in French. "B-D-G became P-T-K."

"Right," said Tom. "But what does that mean?" Silence.

Then we started to babble. B-B-P-P-D-D-T-T-G-G-K-K.

"Wait!" Pauline blurted out. "Over time they became different languages. B-D-G becomes P-T-K!"

In other words: languages sprang from a common source, were transformed, and grew apart while still sharing roots. D turned into T. "Door" in English became "*Tür*" in German. "Deep" became "*Tief*."

I clasped my hands. "One pattern replaces another."

We danced around like the heavens had opened. We were a choir of angels chanting, "B-D-G and P-T-K!"

*≈*

After that day, I saw Jakob Grimm's letters everywhere. And how they could mean many things. For example: My term paper with a red letter B inscribed in a circle at the top. The professor informed me that nobody had ever turned in a term paper so early and suggested revisions to raise my grade to an A-.

"You may not like it," she said in all sincerity, "but defending your words will be a major part of your profession."

In my apartment afterward, I stared at the carved ceiling. I felt no compulsion to rise to her challenge. Just a question playing in my mind: was this truly the life I wanted?

"No." I spoke my answer aloud. "I'm not going to revise it." I jumped up and ran to my bathroom mirror. "Hello!" I said with drama. "I'm Amy Hallberg, PhD." I laughed harder than I had in a long while —as if all the titles in the world would bring me happiness. Although . . .

For one full day, I contemplated med school. Because that's what smart people do if they don't get a PhD. But I never cared for bodily fluids or animal dissection, though I cheered on lab partners as they did the cutting in high school biology. It took a few days longer before I put a name to my dream: Frau Hallberg, high school German teacher. Mom described the profession as noble and good for mothers when I called to tell her. Dad was pleased, having never understood my drive for a PhD anyway.

Once I decided to drop out, I found I wanted to stay through the end of the year. My scholarship covered tuition, I had my monthly stipend, and my lease ran through May. More important, I adored my new circle of friends, all German-speaking transplants to St. Louis.

Several of us met up that winter in an Italian restaurant on the edge of campus. Its owner, a Jewish man, had filled the room with stained glass Jesuses salvaged from old churches. While eating toasted ravioli, I spoke with a man who studied Spanish. "I'm planning to leave at the end of the year," I said, cautious to keep my voice down.

"I can see that," he said without hesitation. "I once studied a cadaver. Dissecting literature is like that. Once you reduce it to its parts, it's not really a person anymore."

"Yes," I said. "That's how I feel."

# 9

## Becoming Frau Hallberg / Frau Hallberg werden

Over the next two years, my life as Frau Hallberg took shape, at a much slower speed. Because I had no experience teaching teens, the U of M licensure program didn't accept me. While I regrouped, Mom talked me into applying for a temporary sub license so I could fill in at my old high school. On the very first day, I was leading a geometry class,when one boy stood up, walked across the room, and slammed another kid against the wall. Though I quickly got to the root of the problem ("He threw a penny at my eye!") and sent both guys to the office, I didn't want to return.

"You can do this," Mom said at home that evening. "Let me tell you a secret. You can't control teens. Fill their buckets on the way in." She nodded, eyebrows raised. "Notice them." By the end of that first year, the teacher in the unruly class had resigned and I had become their long-term math sub, teaching on a variance, following Mom's plans and procedures while taking evening classes. I subbed other subjects too. By June, I knew most of the kids in that school by name, though I had a reputation for being detention happy. I kept order and followed directions and documented everything in meticulous notes to teachers. I did likewise when I student taught middle school German in a neighboring town.

The spring of the second year, I was back in Mom's classroom. I'd earned my German licensure but jobs were scarce and I'd made plans to student teach Spanish. I had just gotten her students' attention when the phone rang in the corner.

"Amy!" Mom sounded exactly like her older sister. "I'm riding to this conference with an English teacher. When I told her about you, she made me pull over."

"I'm teaching your calculus class."

"I know, but listen. Call her principal. Speak with him directly. Today. There's a high school German position just across the river."

It may have been my dream job leading my own program, but the learning curve was steep. On this new-to-me schedule—the block—we had ninety minutes to fill, and my predecessor had left nothing behind except textbooks, not even instructions on how far his classes had gotten. I overestimated and had to regroup right away. Students began schooling me on the ways of Herr B—a brilliant man who had given them hope, then returned to Germany after one year. For example, they'd learn more if I had better posters—like ones he'd given to them. I owned four: the Cologne Cathedral by night, a movie poster for *Feivel der Mauswanderer* ("Fievel, the Wandering Mouse" a.k.a. *An American Tail),* one from the Haus am Checkpoint Charlie ("Where world history manifests itself"), and another for a performance of *Jesus Christ Superstar*—not a poster I could display. Sometimes I'd step into the hall between classes and take several deep breaths. Unlike when I subbed, I couldn't send everyone to the office when they ignored me or smirked. At the end of the day, I often sent myself.

The assistant principal who hired me didn't know German, but Barbara used to teach English, Russian, and Spanish. As busy as she was, Barbara flashed her tremendous grin and found five spare minutes whenever I stopped by. She'd offer five learning strategies off the top of her head, and she didn't care which one I tried. Her ideas worked wonders.

Once Barbara drew a sequence of images with a fine-tip permanent marker: a smiley face, a neutral face, and a frowny face. The pungent ink soaked into the page. My sweetly savvy mentor looked up. "When you learn a language, at first you are so happy. But as you progress, you start to doubt yourself. Until you hit a wall." She drew a vertical line. "At that point you have two choices. You can quit or you can keep going." She fixed her cerulean eyes on me, eyebrows arched, smiling brightly. "The trick is to move past perfection to the place where you let yourself learn."

She drew a second smiley face on the other side of the line and capped her marker. "As long as you keep growing, you'll always have a home here."

ٮ

In those early days, I based many grammar and culture lessons on conversations with Eva.

"You only use *wann* in a question," she once told me while walking through town. "Like 'when will something happen?'"

*Wenn* meant "whenever" or "if." She clarified that point of confusion.

"If something hasn't happened yet, it is only possible, not for sure," She pointed to a café. "*Wenn*, or if, we go there, we could meet Claudi for tea or a cherry Granini. And then there's *als*." Eva paused while I digested all these similar words. "It means 'when,' 'one time,' an action completed in the past."

"But what about *falls?*" I protested. "I thought *falls* meant 'if.'"

"No, that's only in case of . . . like 'in case of emergency.' You use that all the time. But it's not quite right. It's too much drama." It was an old refrain. "Sometimes you try too hard. But when you relax, you're wonderful. So relax and be yourself."

I took those classic lessons to heart. The field trip I led to a German restaurant—in a neighboring town, with much needed assistance from a skillful parent—told me I wasn't prepared for overnight travel with students. But I recruited five students that first year for Eva's and my old exchange, still in operation between Minnesota and Baden-Württemberg.

Barbara walked me through the approval process, including the contents of my proposal and what I should say to the school board. "I see myself in you," she said, helping me assemble packets. "You'll make a great administrator someday."

I laughed and shook my head. "It's enough to work for a woman like you."

"With me," she corrected.

As it turned out, she was right. I'd caught the statewide committee's attention, and they invited me to join them in administering the exchange. From then on, I helped pair partners. A few of my students stepped up every year.

.♀

I kept my feet on American soil, but over those first five years in the classroom, my German expertise—and comfort—grew more robust.

Those exchange students from both sides kept me current on modern German advances. And while teaching, I educated myself.

Every day for grammar instruction, my students and I would take out the *Rosablatt*—meaning "pink sheet." I'd meticulously compiled the hand-printed chart from references—sixteen boxes in all. On the back, I'd composed a series of questions to find the right endings. It had evolved—especially after a favorite student typed it into a document.

Was the noun masculine? Feminine? Neuter? Always I downplayed the term, deadpan; always it got a laugh anyway.

Maybe a noun was plural. There were telltale signs.

And cases: can you find the subject, direct object, indirect object, possessive?

We memorized prepositions to the melody of the waltz "The Blue Danube." *Aus ausser bei mit nach seit von zu,* we sang in repetition.

"Those words force you to follow with dative," I always lectured.

"But what makes them dative?" someone always asked.

In the face of instinct-defying grammar, I turned to a poster above the whiteboard. Jakob and Wilhelm Grimm, masters of German grammar, sat on a stone in a meadow, surrounded by fairytale flora and fauna.

"*Jakob,*" I implored. "*Warum?*" Why? Why is it this way?

He stared back wordless, dead for a century and a half. Jakob only wrote down what he'd observed anyway.

"I don't know why," I admitted. "That's just how it is. You'll have to accept it."

Recognizing patterns made everything else possible. We used them to work our way up not just to simple fairy tales, but to poetry by the likes of Goethe and his pal Friedrich Schiller.

*✐*

If only I could meet a man I admired so well in real life. I might as well have lived in a convent, teaching German in high school. I'd dated some men who by their descriptions should have made me happy. Some spoke German. That never worked out. Even their names felt like warnings.

I came to refer to the handsome medical student as "Death," which in German, coincidentally, was *Tod.* We met right after I'd moved back in with my parents. He was a serious student, and I was a grad school dropout. My brother taunted Todd mercilessly when they met, sensing weakness. After that, Todd wouldn't permit me to mention that I had a brother. ("I did you a favor," Ben said later. He was right.)

Shortly before we broke up, I'd asked Todd where in Spain I should do an intensive language study (my backup plan for teaching in case German fell through). He suggested Seville. Once there, I discovered temperatures regularly topped 100 degrees Fahrenheit in July. He might as well have told me to go to hell.

I'd been teaching five years when *Brett* came back into my life. His name meant "board." As in a rigid, squared-off block of wood. A friend of a friend I'd never really clicked with, he emailed me out of the blue, wanting to practice his German. We fell into some kind of groove doing the "Hokey Pokey" at a local Bavarian bar. He seldom came to visit me. We hung out in his apartment, forty-five minutes away from my home.

I found an English copy of *Demian* on Brett's coffee table a few weeks in. I'd mentioned it was my favorite.

"Oh!" I said, buoyed by his attention. "You read *Demian.* What did you think?"

Brett glanced at the table. "I didn't understand the point."

*❦*

After Brett and I broke up, it occurred to me that, with few exceptions, nearly every guy I'd ever dated shared variations on the same few names. Not only that, they all began with BDG and PTK, the sound shifting letters from Grimm's Law.

This coincidence struck me like a bolt of lightning. Because Ben also started with B. And whether I saw them as good or bad, all the men in my life somehow reminded me of my brother, now conducting research and married to Sondra on the East Coast. As if I were still, even at twenty-nine, seeking my big brother's approval.

I was a tenured teacher and independent woman—Frau Hallberg, not Fräulein Maria, going where she was bidden, and not a princess in need of rescue. I lived in my own house, purchased with a small nest egg from my grandma, five miles down the highway from my parents, close to the school where I once staged a protest. Dad had joined me house hunting. Mom had helped me plant my gardens. Ben had flown in to help us lay rolls of sod and dig holes for trees. Still, the decisions were mine, and I'd paid my mortgage for two years.

I'd chosen a life that made me happy. I wanted a man more like me.

*❦*

Rather than stay in my house all summer, I decided to get a summer job—starting evenings in late May before school let out—and earn some cash at a bookstore. Following one last-ditch date with Brett in July, I vented to a coworker, a stylish woman, while we shelved books.

"It took me half an hour to get there, and he couldn't even go for a short walk?"

"He doesn't sound like a catch," she said. "Have you considered our friend David?"

I followed her gaze to see David peeking around a shelf. He disappeared.

I'd considered David. The first time I saw him behind the information desk—the third of July—I felt oddly compelled to introduce myself. (He'd started on my week off, while I was visiting Ben and Sondra to meet my new niece.) David had dark hair and a chiseled face like a Roman statue. He wore neckties and green button-down shirts that set off his deep green eyes. And from our one brief conversation, I knew he'd dropped out of a PhD program in Classics and was earning licensure to become a high school Latin teacher. He was only home for the summer, living in his parents' basement. His father was a professor.

"You know David's twenty-four, right?" I said.

"My husband's ten years older than me," she said. "I don't think age matters."

"He's too young, and he's going back to school in Wisconsin."

$\mathscr{D}$

David's sticky notes for shelving locations, as determined by computer search, made me laugh. For a book that belonged in "Words on Words," he wrote a Hamlet quote: "Words, words, words." On a book actually called *Words on Words*, he wrote, "Guess."

Over the following month, I made ever-wider laps through the store during my time on shelving duty, collecting as many out-of-place books as I could to dump on his sorting pile. Whenever I did, he locked eyes with me, silently accepting my challenge.

In early August, David joined me at a table in the back room for an afternoon break. The store had recently displayed my staff-recommended book.

"I read *Demian*," David said. "I can see why you like it."

"Really?" My face grew warm. "Did you recommend anything?"

"*The Brothers Karamazov.*"

"Haven't read it. I suppose you have brothers?"

He smiled. "Two brothers, two sisters, three goldens, three cats."

"Your family has five kids?" I said, almost holding my breath.

"I only want two," he said. "No way I'm putting myself through what my mom did."

*Yes!* I thought. Why I cared, I couldn't quite explain.

"I have a miniature poodle," I ventured.

He looked at me sideways. "A poodle?"

"Wolfgang der Hund."

He cracked a crooked smile. "I don't know about poodles."

One morning the *penultimate* week of August (meaning "second to last," David's favorite word)—I got up early to call the bank and gulped down a heaping bowl of Marshmallow Mateys while I waited on hold. They'd made a series of errors in crediting my mortgage payments. The most recent letter threatened foreclosure. At last, I resolved the issue and rushed to work. I shared my frustration with David when I saw him.

"You own a house?" he asked. "How old are you?"

"I'm twenty-nine."

His jaw dropped, and I walked away smiling. But alone at the downstairs cash register, I suddenly felt faint. I sat on a stool and placed my face in my hands. I got up when a customer asked me to call another store. Darkness crept into my periphery.

"I'm sorry," said the voice on the phone. "We don't have the book you want."

"You don't?" I said. Everything disappeared from view.

"Are you okay?" the customer asked.

It was the last thing I heard. Moments later, two managers found me slumped on the counter, regaining my vision. They helped me to a chair. Somebody brought a bottle of orange juice and a chocolate chip cookie. Someone else called my mother. She called them back a few minutes later to say my step-grandpa was on his way for me.

That's when David found me. "Drinking juice and eating a cookie?" he said, smirking. "What, did you pass out?"

"Yeah, I did."

David's eyes widened. He mumbled a hasty apology and rushed away. Ten minutes later, he emerged from the stacks, followed by my step-grandpa. David had waited by the front door. I could only stammer my thanks. Grandpa had a twinkle in his eyes.

"This is my friend, David," I said. "He's my friend."

At the doctor's office we determined that I was fine, but I'd best avoid mounded bowls of sugary cereal with marshmallows for breakfast, especially when I was already stressed. And when I looked up the name, I discovered that *David* meant "Beloved."

☙

The following week, David showed up at the end of my shift wearing green, plaid flannel. He stepped behind the counter of the lower cash register and waited, tipped off by coworkers that if he asked me out, I wouldn't say no. Riding up the escalator, I lost all patience and asked him to dinner instead.

That's when I discovered my true love went by Dave. And he was happy to drive from Madison to the Twin Cities every weekend, to spend time with Wolfgang den Hund and me.

# 10

## A Wedding in Hamburg / Hamburger Hochzeit

In the year 2000, we flew into Hamburg overnight, right after school let out in the Twin Cities. After six years' absence from both Eva and Germany, I could hardly contain myself. I'd never visited Hamburg. From Eva's descriptions in letters and textbooks on my shelves, I knew so much about the city already. The license plates there read HH—pronounced *ha-ha*—for *Hansestadt Hamburg*, a reminder of the city's past membership in the Hanseatic League, allies in the fight against the tyranny of pirates and tariffs since the Late Middle Ages. Eva had first taught me this fun fact, which in turn I shared with my students.

I had other words in mind this time: we're going to a *Hamburger Hochzeit*. Literally a "high time"—*Hochzeit* meant a wedding. Eva's wedding in Hamburg.

I had it all planned. Dad and I would navigate. Mom would marvel at my skill with the language. Dave would get to know them both. Eva and her family would admire my flawless German, my charming fiancé, and my diamond ring. Even her new husband would have to admit that since our first meeting—a stopover on my way to Seville—I'd grown into my German. After the wedding, Dave, my parents, and I would spirit ourselves away to Berlin, heart and soul of the reunited German nation. Everything felt possible in this new millennium.

I loved the laughing sound of HH. Except the joke was on me from the beginning.

,🙢

By the time we arrived in Hamburg that first morning, tension knotted my shoulders. Along the route to our hotel, graffiti covered every concrete surface we passed, outside our bus and then train windows. They recalled the vibrant marks of rebellion that once coated the Berlin Wall. That impulse had since carried over into the rest of Germany.

At last we arrived at the hotel Eva chose for her guests, an old brick warehouse with crisp white walls and sleek décor. I breathed in the safety of German minimalism, at once traditional and fresh, resilient like a fortress.

I told the desk clerk our name, then spelled it in German. I interpreted her reply for Dave and my parents. "Our rooms are in different hallways on the second floor. Up those stairs." I pointed to a doorway. "We'll have breakfast in there. The bar's there too. That's where we'll meet Eva."

Mom stepped up to the desk clerk. "Could you please repeat what you said using English?"

I sighed and rolled my eyes before stepping away. From the time we'd left the plane Mom had done this. I would read signs aloud, translating word for word, and she would say, "I need to understand for myself," then turn and ask directions from random people on the street. Invariably, the stranger would point in the same direction I had. Mom would make a smug face and do just as I'd suggested.

My frustration rose, clenching my throat each time she did this. "Doesn't she know I teach German for a living?" I mumbled more to myself than Dave. "People pay me to use this language."

Upstairs, Dave followed me around our hotel room, indulging me by listening to running commentary on its German traits.

"See, there's the shower nozzle, like a wall phone on a cord."

He nodded and smiled. "Cool."

"We'll sleep under these featherbeds. We each have our own."

None of this was new to Dave, who patiently nodded with each observation. He'd visited Europe more recently than I had. I was merely echoing what Eva taught me ages before.

Her emails suggested we explore the waterfront while she attended her civil ceremony the day before the church wedding. In recent days, she'd repeatedly sent the same message: "When do you think you'll arrive?"

She'd also warned me months earlier. "I can't watch over you if you come for my wedding." So instead of asking what she preferred, I'd brushed aside her question and replied with our general plans, along with my own set of instructions: "We understand that you're going to be busy. Please do what you need to. We'll entertain ourselves."

∅

By midmorning, we wandered cobblestone streets in the Speicherstadt, a row of brick warehouses rising straight up from the canal waters to cast long shadows and leave a chill even under the mid-June sun. Dave and I walked ahead over cast-iron bridges. My parents remained several paces behind.

After an hour, we returned to the hotel, where I fell into heavy, dreamless sleep until a knocking awakened me. I stumbled out of bed and followed the sound to the door.

Alone in the crisp white hallway, a goddess stood dressed in silken amber honey, her auburn curls pulled up and away from her face. As I shook off remnants of dreams, I couldn't place her. Then I threw my arms around my sometime German fairy godmother.

"You're a legally married woman," I managed, bleary-eyed, inexplicably star-struck and stammering in English.

"Yes, I've been to the Standesamt. I am married by the state." Her sweet voice sounded more formal than usual.

I would question this conversation so many times in the days that followed that I would never remember it exactly. Instead of embracing our moment together, I sent Eva away, asking her to give me a half hour. I insisted I would go wake my parents, and we'd meet her in the bar.

$\mathscr{O}$

Forty-five minutes later, Dave and I sat across from Eva and her new husband, their friends clustered around the long table in the hotel's barroom. Eva explained how her parents had finally, a few nights earlier, given Anton permission to use "*du*"—the casual "you"—and their first names. They linked arms and drank champagne to make it official.

Then Mom's voice cut through our conversation. "Amy!" she called from across the room. "I need you to interpret."

My face tightened. All day she'd refused my guidance. Now she wanted help? But I obeyed, to help her speak with my German host parents, whom she'd never met. Almost immediately, Mom wandered off, leaving Dave, Dad, and me with Eva's relatives.

Mami and Papi had whiter hair than I remembered. Eva's younger brother, Heiko, towered above me. His cheeks were still ruddy, but now he was an accomplished scholar. Snippets of conversation wove in and out of focus. Mami offered me her little finger. I thought she wanted to see my engagement ring, but she simply wanted to link fingers, a common German greeting I didn't yet know.

Time slipped away. Suddenly Mom appeared by my side, telling me Eva and Anton were leaving. She'd been talking to Eva the whole time.

"But I never got to talk to her," I protested as they slipped out the door.

"It's too late," Mom said. "You'll see her at the wedding."

♫

At Eva's wedding, I wanted to show how far I'd come from the girl I was in high school. I also hoped for reassurance that no matter the changes, the important things stayed the same.

The morning of the ceremony, we enjoyed my favorite German breakfast: soft boiled eggs standing in cups and spooned from their shells, hard rolls with jam, salami, slices of cheese, tomato, and cucumber, finished with a cup of hot tea. And I relaxed.

By ten o'clock, a taxi delivered the four of us to the chapel, a white stucco building framed in timber. We stood under a canopy of ancient trees where Mom and I admired a black Mercedes with pink roses strung across the windshield. A giant white tulle bow stretched across the trunk. I took pictures from every side.

"It's not their Mercedes," said Eva's aunt, a tall woman I'd met briefly the night before. She approached us wearing an oversized hat, surrounded by wafts of perfume and grandkids. "The car is for the other wedding."

I sat on a bench between her and Mom, Dave standing beside us, while Dad took more pictures. The children chased each other.

Grasping at polite conversation, I said, "It won't be so long until Eva has one of her own." I registered the aunt's puzzled expression and added, "A child, I mean."

Her eyes narrowed. "Well, no," she said. "Five months."

Her words startled me. "What?" Suddenly I was the one at a loss.

Mom's voice dropped down, soft and low. "Eva's pregnant. She's due in November."

The aunt stood and walked away, leaving us to sort it out.

"How do you know?" My voice sounded tiny.

"Eva told me last night," she said. "I was waiting for her to tell you."

The news sent me reeling. First Mom monopolized Eva all night, then she let me walk into her wedding ignorant of this major life development? "Why didn't she tell me?" I sputtered. "Is she at least happy about it?"

"There wasn't time, and I didn't ask. It's her wedding," Mom said, impatient.

I needed context. "Was she planning on telling me, or were you supposed to? What exactly did she say?"

Mom looked puzzled. "She said, 'Amy doesn't know yet.'"

"Think about it." I choked out the words. "When would she tell me? Her wedding's in twenty minutes."

Mom's face hardened. "I honestly don't remember. Amy, this isn't about you."

I got up and stood to the side, fuming. Dave followed.

"How did this happen?" I asked. "I walked straight into it."

"I don't know," Dave put his arm around me. "I don't know."

The heavy chapel doors opened, and the other wedding's guests spilled onto the lawn. I wanted to flee, but I had no car even if I dared. I had to enter the cavernous white space with its sturdy wooden pews.

With my cheeks still burning, I sat beside Dave, flanked by my parents. Mom leaned over and whispered, "Pull yourself together." I forced a smile and held tears at bay, praying I looked more relaxed than I felt.

Eva appeared in the doorway, an angel in a flowing white gown, bearing pearly white calla lilies. She glided past us in time with the harmonies of American gospel singers, clearly the special surprise she had proudly mentioned in emails. I ducked my head when she passed, then watched her walk the whole way.

Eva had been with Anton for seven years and never mentioned children. But I hadn't returned to Germany since meeting him during their university days, after she transferred to med school in Marburg. I'd stayed for a week on my way to Seville.

Since then, Eva had traveled the world with him, to study medicine in Israel and South Africa. They'd visited America, but never Minnesota. *It's too far*, I told myself, but I'd suspected otherwise. In old pictures, he sat by her side and glared at me, sometimes with his fists balled up. So much was up in the air for me then. I'd blamed Anton for crowding us. One night at a party, he told me flat out that Eva didn't know how to make me happy. Which only made me sadder because it was true. Her life kept progressing—with him—while I still felt like the same adolescent. Eva had run out of answers, and I was tired of asking the questions. On that trip to Marburg, I was happiest exploring without either one of them.

Now, at their wedding, I knew even less what Eva wanted. Why had she kept this baby a secret? And more important, why had she told Mom and not me? Maybe it was simply bad timing. Or maybe our friendship had played itself out. If only I'd listened when she knocked on the door. If only Mom hadn't cut in. If only I could unlearn the news until Eva told me herself, if that ever happened.

In my jet-lagged, nerve-addled condition, I'd become surprisingly brittle. I felt betrayed, jealous of my mother, jealous of Anton. And God help me, I felt jealous of Eva's child.

♌

At the park afterward for the reception, I tried to ground myself. At some point, I'd have to talk to Eva. If only Mom would leave me alone. "Smile!" she demanded when Dave went to get me a cup of soup. I cringed, certain everyone could see us waging our battle of wills.

When I finally reached Eva, I blurted out, "Where are you going on your honeymoon?" I knew it was the wrong approach as soon as the words left my mouth. She didn't need to answer my questions, but darned if I wasn't insisting on answers. Why didn't I comment on the musicians, or the lilies, or the delicious soup?

Eva read my mood with precision. "We'll go to Sylt, in the North Sea," she answered, distant.

"Isn't that the island where your family goes?"

Her stricken expression told me I'd still missed the mark, trying to play the expert again. My heart sank.

"Well, I can't go scuba diving in St. Lucia now. I'm pregnant." She abruptly moved on to the next guest. I could barely breathe.

I scanned the crowd and sought out Eva's old friend Claudi, one of few people I knew. Mercifully, she smiled and told me she was getting ready to leave. All the way back to the hotel, I sat in her backseat, second-guessing everything I had said, both German and English. Claudi and her charming fiancé carried on a conversation with Dave and either didn't notice my distress or ignored it.

To be fair, the entire day went perfectly, every part exactly as Eva wanted, except for one miserable American fighting total meltdown. Have you ever heard the advice that at a wedding, you should assume something will go wrong and make a game of it? Then when it does go wrong, you can laugh and say, "Ah, that's what it is!" and ignore it? At this wedding, I was the one thing going wrong. Every mirror I passed told me my fragile expression matched the way I felt: alone.

That evening, Anton stood to make a toast. He spoke of *Gemütlichkeit*—coziness—and a festive atmosphere. After several courses, the speeches began. I understood nothing, except for one witty comment about the pregnancy. I paged through my program to reread the words in the printed text.

When, finally, Eva and Anton got up to mingle, I wanted to tell her how happy I was for her. I desperately wanted to *be* happy. She smiled brightly at Dave and exchanged a few easy words with my parents. When she turned to me, I asked about the kind of stone in her ring. "I don't know," she answered, her expression inscrutable. "Green?"

At midnight, I watched Eva turn on the dance floor with her new husband, a spinning blur. The dancing would go on for hours. Dave ushered me out moments before I dissolved into a blubbering mess. He held me against his chest while we waited in the rain for a taxi. Eva was living her life. That was all.

*❦*

Once, at a party in a wood-paneled fraternity in Marburg, a friend of Anton drew me aside to show me pictures on the wall, generations of young men scarred in duels. Then he pointed to the prominent welt across his own cheek, just below the tiny frames of his glasses. "It's a mark of honor to earn such a scar."

If I'd earned my scars in Germany, Anton had won the battle for Eva's heart. I knew it even in Marburg. Still, I dreamed that one day my children and hers—daughters, perhaps—would continue our friendship where we'd left off. I'd planned to be so gracious at this wedding that Eva and Anton would forget my former childishness. I'd wanted her to recognize the confident educator I'd become. Which was an awfully weighty agenda to ask of any bride at her wedding.

Maybe I could yet regain some dignity and wear my scars with honor. Eva had sent pictures of herself painting apartments with Anton over the years. I wanted to show that, all evidence to the contrary, I'd grown up too.

*❦*

We showed up the next morning for brunch in the garden of Anton's childhood home in a quaint seaside suburb with white brick walls. Eva looked sleek and composed in her black sleeveless dress. I felt short, a frumpy American among giant Germans.

Eva's new father-in-law sat beside me. "You teach German?" He laughed. "Why would anyone bother learning German? All Germans know English."

I excused myself and went to join Eva, who was chatting with Dave.

"I want all my children to learn Greek and Latin," she said, animated, relaxed.

I broke in. "You should send your child to stay with us someday." I sounded needy, and not the least bit gracious. She looked past me.

Later, while I called for our ride, Eva walked into the living room. She told me which buttons to push on my phone and waited until I finished speaking. Then she hugged me goodbye. When she pulled back, she said, "Do you remember the poster you wanted the last time you visited? For your future classroom?"

"An ad for the festival. I'd forgotten about that." We'd drunk *Sekt* in the street—bubbly wine with fruit. We'd laughed and danced with Eva's friends. I'd wanted to run back in the darkness and grab the poster off a door, but we were driving to Donaueschingen early the next morning, and Eva had insisted on going home to bed. Yes, that was a happy night.

"I went back and got the poster for you," Eva said. "It's at my apartment, though."

A mixture of elation and regret washed over me. "That's okay. I don't need it."

"What?" she asked, eyes wide. She gave an ironic laugh. "You said you wanted it. I kept it for you all these years. I took it everywhere I moved."

"Oh." I placed my palm on my burning cheek. "Thanks. You could mail it. But please don't worry about me."

The words didn't say what I wanted at all. I wanted to say, "Thank you. For everything." But it was too late. She was gone.

# II

## Souvenirs from Berlin / Berliner Andenken

Two days after the wedding, we climbed the spiraling incline within a glass and steel dome. Through its framework, I caught glimpses of a modern Berlin. Barely one year old, the orb perched atop the restored Reichstag, crowning jewel to celebrate the German Parliament's overdue return home. *Dem deutschen Volke*—"To the German People"—read the inscription across the building's façade. On my visit to West Berlin in 1987, the words had long sounded an ironic tone, beginning with the mysterious fire that ravaged the Reichstag before World War II.

The Berlin Wall had stood behind it for years. But all that had changed overnight. "November 9, 1989," read the caption of a poster in my classroom, an image of jubilant East and West Germans celebrating into the night, dancing below and on top of the wall itself. I had taught this history my whole career.

Now, in the year 2000, the Reichstag embodied a spirit of gravitas. *To and for the Germans.* As if to punctuate that new reality, mirrors at the core of the sphere reflected everyone walking its winding path. Transparent panels inside the guardrails offered a bird's eye view of the meeting chamber below. Stopping to take it all in, reading every sign in both German and English, I lagged far behind Dave and my parents.

When we reached the base, we stepped onto the terrace for an unobstructed view. My parents walked in one direction while Dave and I headed in the other.

"Can you believe this?" I asked him. "In 1987, there was a museum on one side of this building. The other half was storage space. There's Russian profanity painted on some of the walls."

Dave scanned the city. "Look at all the building cranes."

I nodded. "I thought construction would be further along."

I thought about our early-afternoon walk past the East German television tower at Alexanderplatz, origin of so much propaganda in its day. White canvas banners now draped the scaffolding of the medieval church in its shadow. The signs featured enormous bottles of water with the caption "the ultimate purity" written in English. In a place where once they spoke only German and Russian.

When I explained that context, my parents and Dave nodded and smiled. I longed to be there with Eva, who would've shared my amusement. But Eva was back in Hamburg, packing for her honeymoon. And so I focused all my attention on Mom, whether moving toward her or moving away.

Earlier, we'd taken a break at a café table beside the Brandenburg Gate. I'd tried to impress upon her what it meant to sit in that particular spot and eat ice cream and watch cars drive right through the gate. And not crappy East German cars, but modern German cars.

"Do you like the stuffed bear I bought?" she'd answered. "I think it's cute how it's called *Bärlin*." She said the city's name as it sounded in German, Bear-lean. I'd nodded and smiled, but I hadn't shared her amusement.

"At least I saw the Berlin Wall," I said now to Dave, peering out from the roof of the Reichstag. "My mom will never know what that felt like."

"Right," Dave said, having never seen it himself. But his father had visited Berlin in the days after the slabs arrived. Dave's dad had crossed the border several times in the summer of 1961, just to show he could.

I hadn't known in 1987 how close we were to the end. "I'm glad I was there to witness it," I repeated, looking through my camera, trying to capture those cranes. I resolved to make the most of this time, now.

.℘

The following morning, Dave and I walked along an industrial road in the rain to reach Plötzensee, the execution site I mentioned whenever I lectured on the German resistance. For Dave—and myself—I translated the words across the brick wall that greeted us. "To the victims of the Hitler dictatorship of the years 1923–1945." The wooden doors were closed tight. "I'm sorry," I told Dave. "I thought there was more to it."

"It's okay," he said. "Let's find the sections of the wall. We'll walk past Checkpoint Charlie on the way."

I felt only a flicker of excitement as I passed that famous sign, written in German, English, French, and Russian: *You are leaving the American sector.* We could also read the sign they saw in the East: *You are entering the American sector.* Berlin definitely felt that way to me now.

At last, we reached slabs of the once-formidable Berlin Wall, pockmarked and gray with exposed, sagging steel cables, corroded rolls of metal capping them off. A panel farther down was still intact. I stood before it for a long while. A face with a schism stared back: half black with yellow hair, half red with black hair, the colors of the German flag, all on a black background.

Dave read the words aloud, "*Alles wird besser aber nichts wird gut. Die Freiheit hab ich nicht gefunden vor oder hinter diesen Stein.* What does that mean?"

"'Everything gets better, but nothing gets good. I haven't found freedom in front of or behind this stone.'" I sighed. "I don't know what else to show you."

And so we went shopping at KaDeWe—short for Kaufhaus des Westens, Buying House of the West—the largest department store in continental Europe. We grabbed dinner at their gourmet dining floor and called it a day.

⌒

Back at the Holiday Inn, my parents knocked on our door. "Hello!" Mom said, giddy. "You'll never believe what we bought!"

Dad beamed. "These guys were selling scooters. They looked like so much fun we bought two."

"You rode scooters all day?" I could feel my lips purse.

"We've been exploring all over," Mom said.

"Have you eaten?" I asked.

"Oh yes," said Dad. "We had McDonald's for lunch, Chinese for dinner."

"Of course you have." My throat tightened. "Meet up tomorrow for Potsdam?"

"Trains run every hour. Eva said we can't miss it," said Dad.

After they left, Dave dutifully rolled his eyes and sat on the bed, listening to me rant, softly so they wouldn't hear through our shared wall. Before going to sleep, I unpacked my souvenir from KaDeWe. It was a butter dish, the same porcelain-white color as the wedding china we had chosen back home. This was a little round pool with a domed lid. A tiny duck sat on top as its handle. Our actual pattern was closer to the original scrolling textures of the Reichstag.

The duck seemed freer, less confined. The word *Vogelfrei* came to mind. Free as a bird. In English, it was a good thing. Nobody can cage you, nobody can hold you down. But in German, it meant "without protection or moorings." Out there on the winds that can change at any time. And maybe that bird was me. Finally ready to spread my wings, only to discover I had no perspective at all. Smashing myself against a window that had closed, an outdated era of history.

On the day we visited Potsdam, I resolved to keep the peace and my feelings in check. We walked through narrow cobblestone streets, following posted signs. I did my best to ignore Mom's running monologue about the previous night's waitress.

"Her English was terrible. I pointed at the menu to ask what different things were. No matter what I asked about, the waitress said, 'It's meat. It's very good. You'll like it.'" Mom rolled her eyes and gestured broadly as she told the story. I didn't respond, but inside I judged every word she said. Never mind that the native language was German. I'd quit offering to help her back in Hamburg.

When we arrived outside Sans Souçi—French for "without care" and residence of Frederick the Great, King of Prussia—I looked at the green gates and felt our energy shift. There was something magical about the golden-yellow Rococo villa before us. And this was merely the portal to an entire park full of castles.

A spinning windmill creaked in the breeze. It reminded me of something, and I listened for a while, letting the morning sun relax me.

"Oh!" I said at last. "My students read a story about that windmill."

"Oh yeah?" Mom said.

"It was noisy, but the farmer refused to take it down, so Friedrich let it stay."

Inside the villa's entryway, we fished giant felt slippers out of baskets, big enough to pull on over our shoes. We shuffled across floors of polished stone into rooms with polished stone walls.

While I took in the German tour, my parents and Dave listened to recordings in English. Back outside, we looked out over a perfectly manicured park and a great round pool with a fountain in the center. We descended a majestic set of stairs down the center of a hillside vineyard.

"I can't believe I never knew this was here," I said.

Mom sighed. "Isn't it wonderful?"

Wandering tree-shaded paths, we came upon the Chinesisches Haus. It was a tiny, rounded pavilion painted a robin's egg blue, with swirling designs on its gray roof. Gold leaf covered the decor—four pillars along the front steps, the edging, the ornamentation around every window, statues of Chinese people around the building's foundation, a lone statue shaded by an outspread parasol on the top of the roof.

"It looks like a gilded nest," I said. "Was it really just a place to sip their tea?"

Dave glanced at his guidebook. "It took almost a decade to complete because of the Seven Years' War." He looked up. "I can see why peasants would revolt."

My parents laughed, coming around from the other side. I laughed.

He had a point, of course, but the decadent little teahouse was so alluring. I wanted to hold it in the palm of my hand. It reminded me of another treasure I once brought Mom from West Berlin, a dainty music box. And I suddenly wondered what it must've felt like to Mom, to send me to Germany and receive my dainty treasures when she'd never left the United States. When in fact this was her first time in Germany. It felt good to see her enjoy it.

At the far edge of the park, we approached the *Neue Palais*, an imposing red stucco masterpiece with marble statues stationed all along the perimeter of the roof. Where my parents went, I didn't notice. Dave and I followed a tour for a while, then wandered off to explore. In the ballroom, wide bands of agate and seashells alternated with mother of pearl. In one bedroom, silver embellished every stick of furniture—truly an embarrassment of riches.

Outside in Prussia, the people were starving. And I didn't quite know what to do with this knowledge. But this visit had impressed on me how much I still didn't know about Germany. More important, I was still hungry to learn.

We met my parents outside on the terrace.

"Can you believe this survived two world wars?" Dad said.

"I can't believe the Russians didn't strip it and send the treasures back home," I said.

"I don't think they had money to restore it." Mom pointed. "Do you see how some of those statues look sooty? They must have begun restoration after the wall fell."

It was already midafternoon, and suddenly we realized how hot, thirsty, and hungry we felt. Along the park boundaries, a sign near a hedge pointed us to a small café: a couple lone tables on the patio of a house. The waitress, a middle-aged woman who grew up in East Germany, spoke no English, and the menu had no translations.

"Amy, can you help me read this menu?" Mom asked.

I smiled. "Here's *Schnitzel mit Kartoffeln und Salat*," I began. "That's a pork cutlet with potatoes and salad. I think you'll like it."

℘

On our walk down the boulevard from the familiar Zoologischer Garten station to the Holiday Inn, I savored the tired satisfaction from our surprising day in Potsdam. Another surprise awaited us at the streetside reception window where the hotel held onto room keys. The clerk handed us a phone message. *From Eva,* read the slip of paper. *Thank you for your love.* I felt grateful for the bittersweet reminder.

Even leaving for her honeymoon, Eva was still looking out for us. On our last morning, we made our way to one final site she'd recommended. From the outside, the Neue Synagoge looked like a normal synagogue, a tall brick building with Hebrew lettering across the front and towers like blue Faberge eggs. Only a small bronze plaque explained its significance: *Damaged but saved on Kristallnacht, destroyed during the allied bombings on Berlin.* We had to pass through screening to enter, same as at the Reichstag.

"The security makes sense," Mom said. "Remember the Israeli hostages at the Munich Olympics?" She grew up in a Minneapolis suburb with a large Jewish population, so she'd paid attention to that tragedy in 1972, long after the Holocaust. In that moment, I realized something— she understood this part better than I did.

This museum didn't focus on the KZ atrocities that the world and I knew so well. After all, the horrors didn't begin with mass executions. In this place we witnessed something subtler: reality as found in stories and artifacts. These were testimonials from the everyday lives of German Jews, when the small indignities began: microaggressions, barely perceptible and easy to write off.

That was how the Holocaust started. A gradual progression of disruptions and petty insults, ignored enough times by others. People looking the other way. It started years before *Kristallnacht*. Certainly everything changed that terrible night when Nazis destroyed Jewish property throughout the country. But many everyday Germans barely took notice the following morning. Because the systematic stripping of all dignity and every human right had begun long before then, not afterward with the advent of yellow stars that every Jew had to wear visibly pinned to their outer clothing. And certainly not with the Holocaust the world finally noticed.

This realization made me more uncomfortable than I cared to admit. I suddenly remembered something Eva once said: "You know all about our history. Perhaps you should learn more about your own." It was more an observation than an accusation, but she was deadly serious all the same. At the time, I must've defended myself. Now I let this memory linger as I entered the final room.

It was an empty concrete space that once contained the sanctuary. My parents, Dave, and I stood looking at shards of stained glass and rubble, painstakingly pieced together to create a fragment of the original stained glass wall. The silence echoed in the cool, still air. A gray outline of the missing pieces filled in the gaps.

I had no words to describe what I felt. With my beautiful souvenirs, what did I know of suffering? I knew nothing of losing friends and family and starting over. Nothing at all.

How dare I forget that, alone as I had felt in Hamburg, I was surrounded by family: parents who raised me to believe I could do anything, a friend who took time to send her love, and this man who promised to share my life. Nobody had abandoned me. The time had simply come to leave the nest, to learn what it meant to soar free.

# 12

## Happy Little Dolls / Glückliche Püppchen

The first full-length book I assigned my German students to read was a simplified version of *The White Rose*. Written by Hans and Sophie Scholl's older sister, it tells the story of how White Rose leaflets appeared throughout Southern Germany—and in Austria and Hamburg and Berlin—before Sophie was caught at the University of Munich. Condemned days later with Hans and their friend in a speedy trial, their insistent voices made Nazis panic. They were beheaded before sundown.

What made me saddest about this story, ever since I first heard about Sophie, was that she missed out on a husband and kids. She completed her compulsory service during the war, a teacher longing for kindred spirits, finding solace in music and nature. But she never saw her fiancé again. He would return from the Russian front and marry her younger sister instead. It seemed so unfair. And still, after all she'd lost, in the moments before her death, Sophie proclaimed, "What a beautiful day, and I must go. The sun still shines."

Perhaps that sadness explains my response when I stepped into the office at school and looked up at the TV to see not one, but two planes crash into buildings and burst into flames. It was September 11, 2001.

Not two months earlier, Dave and I had flown home from a honeymoon in Sweden and England.

I ran to call Mom, fretting that I might never have children. The world had changed.

Mom, whose birthday fell on that same day, was despondent herself, but this struck a chord with her. "Don't you talk that way," she said. "You sound like my mother, complaining that she brought me into a terrible world. I was a little girl. I deserved better."

I heaved a great sigh. "You really think we'll move past this?"

"Never you worry. Twins run in our family." She meant her Swedish Grandma Amelia, who buried infant sons in the Old Country. "Now there was a woman who knew about heartbreak. Widowed and penniless in America. The orphanage came for her five children and she refused to let them in. She barely spoke English. And do you remember what Amelia said when she closed the door? She said, 'Be it ever so bad, it's good for something.' Amy, we'll be fine."

Mom referred to Amelia often, including the part about twins. That's why, early in my pregnancy in 2002, I asked the doctor to check for a second heartbeat. She didn't find it. She also didn't try very hard. At our twenty-week ultrasound, the technician looked at the screen and said, "There are two of them in there."

As the beings came into stark focus, my stunned mind jumped to our single stroller, high chair, and crib.

"This one's a girl," she said, pointing. "And this one is too."

Dave leaned toward my ear. "We won't have to argue over who's getting up at night," he murmured. "We both will."

I looked into those comforting green eyes, and we held each other's gaze. By now he had his own teaching job, resurrecting a tiny remnant of a Latin program at a different district across the river. He was also taking classes to complete his English certification. I couldn't see how the two of us would ever manage on our own, but I wanted those unexpected twins with a hunger I'd never known.

We drove to show Dave's mom the printout first. An easygoing mother of five, she'd promised to care for the baby she'd asked for since our engagement.

"Fuck!" she said, staring at two heads in profile. "I agreed to watch one baby."

At my parents' house, Mom shouted, "Yes!" and danced around the kitchen. "I told you twins run in my family. You'll need a double stroller. Your grandma will buy a second crib. I'll get another highchair." She'd buy a second set for her house as well, already decked out for one grandbaby.

Our new doctor for an upgraded high-risk pregnancy peered over the top of her glasses at our first appointment. "When I put you on bed rest, you'll go straight home. July would be tragic. August is better. We're aiming for September." It would take nearly that long to find a substitute teacher for my classes.

After school ended in late June, I retired to our living room sofa for long stretches of reading and TV watching. Even walks to the end of our street winded me and driving made me edgy. While I rested, Barbara—ever my faithful mentor—sought candidates she deemed qualified to safeguard my classes. She consulted with me at every step while savoring details about my twin pregnancy whenever Dave's mom drove me to sit in on interviews.

On the day we hired the sub, Barbara gave me two painted sets of German china. One showed Cinderella, seated beside her open kitchen window, surrounded by birds. The other depicted Sleeping Beauty, slumbering under a rose tree in full bloom. Both princesses, within sight of the castle, dreamed of the future, like me.

"Your German program is your first baby." Barbara watched me to make sure I understood. "I'll look after it for you."

✵

By August, Mom delivered audiobooks so I wouldn't have to sit up in bed, crossword puzzles to engage my brain, yarn to crochet into baptismal gowns—everything she could think of to keep me comfortable while I lay in waiting. After Dave returned to his teacher's workshop the week before school started, one of our moms brought me lunch every day.

In the wee hours before the first day of school that fall, our first daughter's water broke, sending me into labor. (The second twin was hanging tight in her own sac, having wrestled to turn her head upward, away from her sister.) Mom missed teaching on the opening day of the new local high school, and Dave scrambled to prepare substitute plans.

At the end of the day, while nurses wheeled me off—alone—to a recovery room, freshly wounded by the Caesarian delivery of our second twin, Dave accompanied both girls to the intensive care nursery upstairs for observation. That evening, while nestled against my tiny firstborn daughter, I took a call from my own substitute, seeking advice about a student I didn't know. In subsequent days, someone else answered the phone.

Nobody left me alone after that.

Our mothers came to the hospital in shifts. Starting on the third day, Dave left for school in the morning, and I stayed on. Mira and Olivia were so tiny, our barely five-pound daughters cocooned in blankets. We weighed them and pumped milk into their stomachs via tubes through their noses. We wheeled clear plastic bassinets to the NICU and back down the hall, where passing visitors gushed over them, never noticing our need for space.

Near midnight that night, Dave and I watched Mira lying under blue lights to fight off jaundice, eyes shielded by a neoprene mask attached to Velcro dots.

"She looks so peaceful," I said. "Will we get to bring her home soon?"

At the sound of my voice, Mira raised her tiny hands and slowly pulled her beanie cap over her eyes. She curled her hands into her sleeves and crossed her arms in front of her face. I felt my fragile energy deflate.

"Is she okay?" I pleaded with the nurse on duty.

"She's overstimulated," the nurse said. "She'll be fine."

Back in my room, I wanted to pull the covers over my face and hide from my own mom's cheerful voice. She arrived at the hospital each evening, face expertly painted, sleek hair framing earrings to match her outfit, ready for pictures with her granddaughters. And she'd taught all day. Around that same time, like clockwork, exhaustion reduced me to tears.

"You're not nice to me," she snarled one week in. "I'll never have any other local grandchildren." She stared me down, daring me to answer.

"This is my only chance too, as a mother," I said, barely able to think. I'm not sure what she expected, seeing disheveled hair and pale, drawn face. I wore Birkenstock sandals adjusted for my puffy feet. A loose floral dress floated over my scarred, bloated belly. That's what I saw in the mirror when I shuffled downstairs to buy her a present. TV footage of plane crashes had reminded me it was September 11, or I would've forgotten her birthday as well.

In the Catholic hospital gift shop, I stared at a display case of rosaries and crosses, silently sobbing. At last I bought a pewter prayer box on a chain. Mom could open the latch and slip a paper inside with the names of all her grandchildren on it. I hoped that would be enough. Because of course I felt guilty. I had the two healthy babies I'd always wanted. People kept telling me I should be happy—or at least stable.

The nurse who taught our parenting class found me fretting afterward. "You're not okay," she said, enveloping me in a bear hug. "You just gave birth to premature twins. You're not supposed to be okay." She gave me a sleeping pill for a few hours' release.

⚘

In a green and pink stained-glass frame in my living room, I had a black-and-white photo, taken when Mom and her closest sister were young. They stand side by side in their front yard surrounded by a picket fence. Each girl holds a doll as if to display rather than nurture it. My mother, dark haired, wears a tentative smile. My aunt, blond and a head taller, scowls. Most of their dolls were paper dolls. In fact, their oldest sister once bribed me with paper dolls to shut me up. I can only imagine how she treated them.

No grandmother ever nurtured them. I was grown before Mom

realized she'd named me after the wheelchair-bound woman who smiled and murmured a few words of Swedish when they met exactly once in a nursing home parking lot. So it shouldn't have surprised me that Mom had her heart set on a happier ending this time.

.℘

Grandmas arrived at my house on a regular basis. We desperately needed their help to get by.

Mondays through Fridays, Dave's mom came at six in the morning. After my mom finished teaching, she showed up in the afternoon for two hours until my weary husband returned from teaching, which—I not-so-secretly suspected—came as a welcome reprieve. "Changing of the Grandmas," our moms called it when they crossed paths. Only a few other relatives had access to our house: A cousin's wife on Dave's side came every Tuesday and cooked us dinner. On weekends my grandmother and step-grandpa stopped by with boxes of food wrapped in tinfoil. While relatives held my babies, I rushed around shoving laundry into machines and washing dishes, when I wasn't nursing both twins at the same time. To minimize the distinctive feeling of life in an open-air freak show, I kept all other family at bay.

Our children wouldn't let us set them down for a moment. Dave and I would trade one wailing infant for the other when we couldn't take it anymore—at least it was a different child. Even when we slept, their muffled cries rang over the monitor, drowning out recorded melodies. Finally, Dave and I started holding one baby each all through the night. They really only settled down entirely when I fed them, for as long as my body could manage.

All our nerves were frayed. Mom alternated between support and dismay. And then her sister, Vivian, flew into town.

"I'll help you all weekend with your babies," my favorite aunt had promised over the phone. She had a way of sounding so sunny. I forgot she shone on her terms.

When Vivian breezed into my house Thursday evening, Mom dropped off an empty plastic laundry basket. She rushed off with another, overflowing with sour onesies and blankets. She would return the load later, smelling sweet and perfectly folded. My aunt stayed behind. I sat slumped in the same corner recliner where I spent every night with a restless child in my arms.

"Let me see my great nieces," Aunt Vivian cooed, peering at each tiny infant. Within an hour, she'd begun pacing.

Because she'd promised to arrive bright and early on Friday, my mother-in-law had made plans for a needed day off. Long after Dave had left, Mom drove up, already late for school, and delivered Aunt Vivian to my doorstep. She spent most of the day out on the back deck. By the time Mom returned after school, my aunt had concocted an important mission for Saturday.

♂

The shadows had grown long before they showed up Saturday evening. The two of them huddled beside the kitchen counter, rustling plastic.

"Come see what we got!" Mom said, elated.

With a colicky infant in my arms, I drew close and counted twelve plastic bags with tiny dolls inside.

"They're Madame Alexander Happy Meal dolls," said my aunt.

Mom continued, enchanted. "We tracked them down at McDonald's all over the Twin Cities."

Words escaped me. The bags contained a winged fairy and Rapunzel with her pink princess hat. There was a girl in a yellow slicker with a ducky hat, girls in leopard and pumpkin and ladybug costumes. Beautiful dolls with rooted hair, painted faces, and movable eyes. Beside the new finds they placed eight more dolls, collected a year earlier and retrieved from Mom's house: Red Riding Hood, Peter Pan, bridal couples. Twenty dolls in all.

Then they pulled pacifiers from a shopping bag, tearing open their cardboard packages, dunking them in boiling water, lining them up beside the dolls. I counted seventeen pacifiers in every color and shape, never mind that these children had never accepted one. "You haven't tried enough kinds," my aunt said.

How I pushed against the rage that stiffened my neck and my arms. How I envied my mom and her sister, trapped as I was, unable to escape for even one day. More than that, I longed for a visit from someone who didn't try to fix this or judge me because it was hard. Because they gave me what they'd most wanted, but they never asked me what worked best for me. Because none of us had a clue what that was.

Not long after Auntie Vivian flew home, I discovered I could calm one daughter at a time by walking in circles, bouncing her in my arms to any song with a rhythmic beat: an Irish jig, an African tribal dance, a Russian folksong played on balalaika. Dave would walk the same way with the other girl.

We still couldn't ever set them down.

꧁

I used to wonder what Red Riding Hood's mother was thinking, sending her daughter off through the forest to Grandma's house, armed only with a basket of goodies and a cape, ill-prepared to meet up with wolves.

When I became the mother of twins, I understood. I was an independent person suddenly reliant on others, caged in so many ways. I returned to teaching after Thanksgiving to help Dave pay for the roof over our heads. But even familiar work overwhelmed us when we cradled babies until dawn, when at last his mother showed up. I survived thanks to notes in my pockets, breadcrumbs to lead me through my days.

Sometimes, even breadcrumbs weren't enough. What I really wanted when family visited was to be a child myself. To be seen and told, "This is hard, but we love you. We know you're strong. You don't have to pretend."

And sometimes I wanted to escape—not my daughters but myself. I wanted to fling my notes to the wind and wander free among the trees, picking every flower I saw, farther and farther from the path. I wouldn't forget it was there; I only wanted to leave for a while, to go out and meet that she-wolf and look her in the eyes. I'd see myself reflected there, and know I was still alive.

*❧*

Outside in the real world, other relatives had waited patiently to meet our twins. Also, Ben's family was coming to town for Christmas. So I arranged a baptism at our church and let Mom invite all the relatives to a coming-out luncheon in the party room at Grandma's condo.

No sooner had I given my permission than a life insurance nurse stopped by our house to run some tests. She took one look at our twins and told us we should skip Christmas. Other people might infect them.

"You need to keep those babies home," the nurse said. "Otherwise, the results could be tragic." Her words stunned me. I thought of my lookalike niece, Selena, so much like me at age five, and eager to meet her new cousins. There was also her tow-headed brother, Jason, always in perpetual motion. They came to town so seldom—I found my own compromise.

After surviving Christmas festivities by keeping ourselves at a distance from people wherever we went, I dreaded the baptism. As soon as the minister spoke the words and touched water to quivering foreheads, we snuck out to another room.

By the time we arrived at the party room, my stomach felt hollow. Dave and I surveyed aunts and uncles and cousins, children racing in circles, voices blanketing the space, all awaiting turns to coo over our twins in white baptismal gowns with white satin slips, opaque white tights, and crocheted booties.

I startled at every approach, wary of noises, germs, and people grabbing tiny hands. Grandma, fighting a lingering cough and stuffy nose, hid in the kitchen.

Finally, when we'd eaten and stayed long enough, Dave and I summoned his cousin's wife, Nina, to help us bundle the girls. I'd welcomed her into our house on many evenings, letting her see me at my most vulnerable. I invited Nina's advice, even though she had no kids. I was grabbing my coat when my seething mother approached.

"That woman won't let me hold my grandchildren."

"I asked Nina to get the kids ready." I avoided all eye contact. "We need to leave. Now."

"I want a picture of Dave's and your grandmas holding the twins."

I cradled my forehead in my palm. "Grandma's sick. She's not touching my babies."

"We'll drape Grandma in a blanket." Mom's stare bore down on me.

"They're old. If we don't do this today, one of them might die. It'll be just like Cora. You'll regret it."

This wasn't a fair comparison. I'd never spoken with my step-great-grandmother about her active Holocaust denial, but I'd planned to confront her with evidence when I got back from West Germany in 1987. Oh, and bring her heart-shaped chocolates that said "*Ich liebe dich*," on the box—meaning to say I love you.

I was just getting around to arranging a visit, the week following my return to America, when Grandma called to say Cora had checked herself into the hospital and died. God help me, I felt a stunned sense of relief. Cora's death kept me from saying something I'd regret. As I might now, if I kept talking, surrounded by all my well-meaning relatives. Such as: this power struggle was about Mom's dead grandma, not mine.

Instead, I closed my eyes. "Fine."

After a few pictures, we grabbed the babies, who were screaming at full lung capacity. They bellowed all the way home, where I stripped them down and threw their gowns into the washer before we bathed them. They were still crying hours later when Nina called.

"Amy, that was not okay," she began.

Relief swept over me. "I know. Can you believe that?"

"You have to protect your children from your relatives," she said firmly. "Those little girls are people. And you're their mother. You have to put your foot down."

I couldn't breathe. I stammered some weak response and got off the phone.

# 13

## Dreams of the Forest / Waldträume

I understood motherhood would change my life. I felt grateful for help that materialized without us even needing to ask. I just never expected so many conflicting emotions, or how much I would dream of a purpose beyond mere survival.

I hungered to play with my daughters. I longed to reconnect with friends and family. Every precious outfit and each adorable toy that arrived in the mail reminded me: someone was rooting for us. But I had no idea how to ask for what I really wanted. For the first time in my life, I couldn't express it in words.

Eva must've understood that feeling. She couldn't come to our wedding when her firstborn daughter was an infant, though she'd tried to make it work. Now, months after giving birth to her second daughter, Eva sent two charcoal jackets, boiled wool with wooden buttons from the Black Forest—miniatures of a jacket I once brought back for Ben. He'd left it behind in a bar almost immediately, leaving both him and me heartbroken. Eva would remember that because she'd helped me pick out the first one. When Ben showed up in Europe the following year, she'd also helped him find its replacement.

These little jackets for Mira and Olivia hinted at a promise I understood. Embroidered with a red script *O* and a bright green *M*, they dwarfed my tiny twins. Not meant for now, but a glimpse at the future.

During a handful of visits to Germany—four times spanning thirteen years—Eva and I followed an unspoken pattern. At some point, I'd wander off on my own, sometimes indulging cravings for adventure, often so I wouldn't smother her. I still found my way home to her, but on each successive visit, I found it increasingly difficult to locate that path back.

By the time my girls were born, I'd nearly given up hope Eva and I would ever find ourselves in the same place again. I couldn't imagine how I'd arrange a meeting between our children in their formative years. But when I saw those jackets, for a fleeting moment, I believed it was possible. Someday . . . after I caught up on sleep . . . when I no longer spent lunchtime pumping milk in a closet and no longer nursed my twins as soon as I got home.

*✣*

One afternoon in the New Year, I begged a few extra hours from Mom so I could go to the auditorium and listen to a life coach talk about balance.

The bubbly coach passed each of us two chocolate kisses and a paper plate. "Eat the first kiss fast," she said. "Notice the amount of pleasure you take from it." Then she instructed us to savor the second. It seemed to me that with every moment spoken for, I didn't have the luxury of savoring anything.

Next, she asked us to write on our plates something we planned to release, something that no longer fit who we were. I realized I wasn't that girl who discovered Germany's history through Eva's eyes and unleashed her own free spirit exploring its landscape. Nor was I that young woman who pored over German literature, decoding it, delighting in sharing the meanings of words. Instead, I found freedom in leaving my house. In German itself, I found obligation—striving not for perfection, or even excellence, but simply lack of catastrophe. And no real connection to my real life.

We stood in a circle up front. When my turn came I spoke in a rush. "I used to be accomplished." Tears spilled down my cheeks. "Now I'm a mother of twins, and that's all over. So, I surrender accomplishment."

I tore my paper into pieces and then watched scraps fall by my feet. Nobody spoke in the awkward pause that followed, as if I'd sucked all the air from the room. A moment later, the activity resumed, but I wasn't listening.

Afterward, the life coach sat down in the row beside me. "You say you're not accomplished," she said. "But how is a mom not accomplished? Think about all you do. It's a different kind of accomplishment."

I stared at my lap, protesting halfheartedly, nearly suffocating under her words. I desperately wanted to believe her. The life coach had other plans that day, but she stayed an extra forty-five minutes, until the milk in my chest felt ready to burst.

"I have to go home now," I said at last, grabbing my bags, thanking her profusely before rushing out the door. I would never see her again. I told myself I didn't have time. Honestly, she terrified me, seeing my vulnerability and reframing it as strength.

I remembered her lesson, though—accomplishment would look different now.

By the girls' first birthday, I'd settled into my role as their mom. Plastic toys lined every wall of our house. On warm Sunday afternoons, we pulled capes over their heads and sent them into the backyard with tiny rakes to scoop up leaves and pluck dandelions. We sang little songs and celebrated small wonders in our circumscribed life. The girls and Wolfgang wandered along shrubs grown tall inside our picket fence.

I noticed how much our garden recalled German backyards I once knew: private and lush and self-contained. For the time being, we were content within our small world.

Upstairs in the girls' closet, those oversized charcoal jackets waited. I didn't know if my daughters would ever see the real Black Forest. And yet . . . every time I looked at those jackets, I could picture our four daughters—Eva's and mine—wandering cobblestone streets together, as we once did. I still had no idea how, though. By this point, even our old Minnesota/Baden-Württemberg exchange program had suffered a lingering demise following 9-11, under the burden of added red tape. Admittedly, by the time we'd met for our final lunch meeting, I was so busy navigating motherhood, I was ready to let go. And that was the only travel option I'd ever offered my students.

And so, in the spring of 2005, when my daughters were eighteen months, I learned how to drive the school activity bus, practicing by driving through a neighborhood half a mile from school. I'd decided to sign up for German Fest, an event held at an immersion camp in north-ern Minnesota. My most accomplished students would speak German all weekend and showcase their talents in competition. I convinced a mother who knew no German to stay overnight at the camp. That way I could sleep in a hotel with my family. Dave and his mom followed the bus in our new minivan, twin toddlers buckled into car seats. We communicated by walkie-talkie; Mira cried only once, when someone turned up the volume too loud.

Though cautious driving the bus, I felt alive. When we reached the turnoff into the woods, I was practically elated. At the camp's entrance stood a replica train station, topped by a clock tower, scaled down from a real one in Germany. I watched everyone take it in. I took a deep breath and exhaled. For the first time, I felt successful as a teacher and mom.

After we parked the bus in the station's shadow and students found their bunks, several joined my family as we wandered through the woods. Once night fell, my tiny children swayed to metallic techno with teenaged students on a patio outside the half-timbered lodge. When we drove the minivan to our hotel, the sound rang in our ears. I couldn't stop smiling.

I had such high hopes that first day. Too high, if I'm being honest.

It took longer than I expected to return to camp in the morning. Without my presence, little things went wrong. Several students missed competitions. And I felt torn: I cajoled them to speak more German, but I also felt obliged to include the non-German speakers along for support.

When a camp counselor explained in German how to clear the dishes from our lunch of *Bratwurst* and *Spätzle*, little Olivia cocked her head and said, "Blah, blah, blah!" The rest of our table laughed—my mother-in-law and Dave and the chaperone. I worried that I had overreached.

I yearned for the time when I could join a party under cover of darkness, on the edge of the real Black Forest. When I could speak German to any number of strangers whose names I would know before I left, and who, for days afterward, would seek me out to offer precious souvenirs. At seventeen, I could slip into the house after the lights were out and sneak upstairs, keeping an eye out for the jealous dog, to let Eva know I'd returned safely. Those youthful escapades, so far removed from my life as a teacher and mom, called me like sirens.

And yet . . . a dozen of us made it to Northern Minnesota and back safely. So what if everything wasn't quite perfect? My team won the trivia contest.

On our way out of the wooded grounds, I took a turn onto a narrow road without an exit and had to back up, which I did, weaving back and forth onto the grass. *Don't back up, if you can help it!* echoed the instructions I had received. *Beep! Beep! Beep!* went the bus. *Go, Frau!* called my students, laughing.

Finally, I did a three-point turn onto the grass and drove out facing forward. Everyone cheered. I had no choice but to laugh. Because it was a start, and if this was the worst that happened that weekend, I was incredibly lucky. And grateful.

And on another level, that ersatz German forest reawakened an acute hunger for something still more authentic. I wanted to introduce my daughters and students to real *Schwarzwälderkirschtorte*—Black Forest Cherry Cake—layers of dark chocolate and whipped cream with sour cherry filling, a ring of cherries circling the top, made by someone's real German grandmother and eaten in Germany while conversing in German.

*ℰ*

Despite the roomy sunroom we loved, our house felt cramped by the time the girls were two. By then, Dave had a tenured full-time Latin and English position, and a higher salary. We were building a larger house a few miles from the old one, overlooking a pond on the edge of a forested wetland. Except for German travel, all my dreams were coming true.

And then one day, out of the blue, an email arrived in my school inbox. A stranger named Julia, an English and Latin teacher, had found me through an Internet search. Julia knew Minnesota. Was I interested in an exchange between our schools? She and her colleague Sabine would walk me through it.

Julia would stay with us. In our new house, we could offer her the whole basement. And my family—all four of us—could stay in her sizable basement in return. Her husband agreed—I could sit in their sunroom between our adventures and write. In their fenced-in garden, our spirited girls could roam free without harm. Julia noted that her grown daughter once ran away to the garden shed for an entire day before coming back inside.

They lived in Karlsruhe, in Baden-Württemberg, where Eva's parents still lived on the edge of the Black Forest. And I remembered Karlsruhe. The forested grounds of a butter-yellow palace occupied its exact center. Streets emanated from it like sun rays. A nobleman named Karl had dreamed the city up—literally. He rode into the countryside and took a nap in the field. Later, he built the palace on the spot, following plans laid out in his vivid dream. He named his refuge Karl's Rest, which took an ironic twist. After city planners razed the church in the Marktplatz where Karl was interred, they left his body in place and erected an honest-to-goodness pyramid. From there, my students could catch trains that would take them anywhere in the surrounding area.

♈

I responded with caution to Julia's email. I asked all the right questions and checked her Minnesota reference. I discussed the idea with Dave and my parents. Looked into school district and immigration policy. These students were classified as three-week visitors and wouldn't actually enroll, meaning we could avoid red tape. But deep down, I'd known my answer immediately. Eva couldn't help me now. My beloved Barbara had moved on. This was my alternative to going it alone. At long last, I would show my students and daughters where Germany existed, beyond the bounds of make-believe. And my family could sneak off to the Black Forest, a couple hours south by train. We started making plans.

That year, I sent Julia and Sabine my family's Christmas photo, taken outside our new house across from the woods: Dave stood beside me, grinning three-year-old daughters perched on our arms, wearing those charcoal-gray jackets that finally fit.

# 14

## Hiking the Pfalz / Pfalzwanderung

On the fifth of July 2009, I celebrated a strange kind of freedom. I'd gotten my group to Germany despite a mess of bureaucratic American logjams. The irony wasn't lost on me. I had plenty of time to reflect during a two-hour road trip up the western edge of Germany, watching wipers sweep rain off our windshield.

Never before had I registered, on an emotional level, all these bridges and valleys, this German patchwork of places. Academically, I knew this context after teaching German fourteen years.

For generations this land existed as individual principalities, from the Reign of Charlemagne, beginning in 800 AD. There was no common German language among them for seven centuries after that. At best there were related dialects until Martin Luther wrote his German Bible. And while inventing the earthy words to express his spiritual understandings, Luther sparked more German discord. Now, seeing the bridges, it made sense—how could people communicate if they never spoke face to face?

The rain had slowed to a constant drizzle by the time we entered the Pfalz. Following closely behind the car driven by Julia's husband, Hugh, we parked our rental on a vineyard slope, beside rows of golden-green vines carefully woven through trellis. Julia, Hugh, and their two friends emerged.

"That's where we'll return for dinner." Julia pointed to the lodge at the base of the hill. "We'll be back in a couple hours."

We nodded and trailed them under the wet sky. They marched past the cars to where the grassy road dissolved into a rusty dirt path. A sharp turn led into forest. Dave and I spurred on our daughters, now nearly six. I had no clue where we'd end up. Julia had invited us, and we came, on retreat from my thirteen students, who were spending their first weekend with Karlsruhe host families.

Olivia and Mira dawdled, Dave sighed audibly, and I stumbled on a stone here, a root there. We'd catch up farther along. We might never make it there again.

*⌒*

By the time Julia came into my life, not only had Barbara moved on but so had all my early champions in leadership positions. Still, I never anticipated so many troubles arranging my second exchange. I did everything by the book, as Barbara taught me.

Julia and Sabine had just sent application packets from twenty-one carefully screened German teens for me to pair with American hosts. On instinct, before I started recruiting, I double-checked with the district to be safe. That's how I found out the policy had changed: to limit liability, school sponsorship for travel was revoked.

Not that I didn't have options. I could—and would—still host guests at school in the fall. And I could recruit students for private travel, under my own insurance. But if anything happened, they told me, I could lose our house. Our new house, overlooking the pond, where I was painting the walls any colors I liked. I panicked.

It would take another year to work up my courage again, with much persuasion from Julia when she brought her group over and stayed in our basement. She read the girls German stories at bedtime, in between herding and caring for twenty-one German teens with Sabina. They would bring a second group over before my one small band of travelers set foot on German soil.

᠑

We were on the verge of leaving America when the unthinkable happened. On the last day of school, while packing up boxes for a reshuffling of classrooms, I received an email: "They are reassigning you to teach middle school Spanish," wrote a colleague. The news had leaked from a backroom meeting. I recoiled reading the words, a slow-motion punch to the gut.

This was *my* German program, built from nothing! Mine to nurture, from the time of my hiring. I was Frau Hallberg, the true German teacher, with German expertise and seniority. Everyone knew that.

I don't know how I got out of the school. I crossed the river in stunned disbelief and somehow found myself back home.

I'd completed my dual-certification as a safety net, to ensure I'd have a job. Barbara had encouraged me, recognizing an influx of administrators talking reform and innovation, hinting at German's diminished value in the world. She wanted me to be safe. And so I had retaught myself what I once knew of Spanish while student-teaching second-year Spanish during my prep time, in a colleague's classroom.

I wrote elaborate Spanish scripts. Otherwise my mind went blank. I continued scripting myself in the inner-city classroom where I student taught native Spanish-speaking third graders at an immersion summer school. I helped them with reading and math skills; they helped me with Spanish. The experience confirmed what I knew: German was my language, and younger kids weren't a good fit. I would never voluntarily give up this position I still loved. Not to help them cut another position elsewhere, nor to make room for a teacher hired after me and not originally for German.

Once I got past the numbness, I raged. I howled. I sobbed. Dave and our terrified girls offered sympathy and left me to my meltdown, closed in behind my office door. During those nightmarish couple of days, I sent fevered emails to every administrator—those I knew, those I didn't. Anyone who might stop this thing from happening. My obsessive rambling swung between profound sadness and outrage. I detailed why this wouldn't work, why they had to find another way, reason piled upon reason. Without me, what would happen to the German program? To the students who loved German as I did? Without them, who was I, the woman who'd built an entire life around this passion?

Vague messages of regret came in response. Finally an email came from the middle school principal: "We are not considering you for Spanish. We will find another option."

Nobody could offer further details. I held on to scant, grasping hope for a solution I could live with when I returned.

$\mathscr{O}$

In the final weeks before our departure, I felt as if I might never breathe deeply again. Could I really get thirteen teenagers and my family of four to Germany and back in one piece? The last visit still weighed on me, when even Mom wouldn't take my advice. Who really believed I could keep up with native speakers? People from one valley to the next didn't understand each other's dialects. And could I really get this whole group through customs and a crowded international airport to a train station via a maze of tunnels I'd never seen? And then there was added pressure because so much was riding on this trip. So many people were watching.

But we made it to the station. Found the right track even. And then, while I searched for a restroom, one of the boys ordered a beer, the first move he made in Germany. I returned to find Dave waiting, holding the golden plastic cup—no, posing—smiling too big, anticipating my measured panic.

"What have you done?" I asked, trying to keep my voice calm. I'd told parents I would send students home for drinking, even if German laws allowed it.

A seasoned teacher himself, Dave took a swig and tossed the cup in a garbage can. His eyes sparkled. "You have your kids well trained," he finally said. "Josh handed me the full cup, terrified and begging forgiveness."

Josh. My wild card. His mother had asked if I really wanted to bring him along. When I tracked him down, Josh told me the rest of the story: meaning to order a bratwurst at a food stand, he sounded out the words at the top of the menu, handed over his money, and took the beer in stunned silence. The story made perfect sense. That sign would confuse a kid just off the plane. But Josh had also fixed his mistake and made a connection with Dave. At this realization, I took a deep breath. Everything would turn out all right.

(Years later Josh would confide that he did take a sip before handing the beer off. This was real German beer, after all.)

We all got onto the right train car after that, all seventeen of us with all our bags, in exactly two minutes. We found our seats and grabbed bags as an assembly line, passing them forward and hoisting them onto overhead racks as the train pulled away from the station. Finally we all sat down, Dave and I each with a daughter, a few rows apart.

As we settled in for the ride, I looked at the woman seated across from Mira and me. A gentle, white-haired woman, she smiled with a knowing eye. "You have quite a group here." She nodded toward the aisle.

I felt keenly aware of Mira and Olivia observing me from their seats, along with this mismatched group I'd pieced together myself.

"Mira," I coached, "Can you speak some German?"

She tucked her chin but peeked up. "*Guten Tag. Ich heiße Mira.*"

Students interrupted now and again, calling out "Frau, Frau!" As Karlsruhe drew closer, my companion looked deep into my eyes, as if offering a benediction. She left the train one stop before our own, where a large group of families already waited to greet us on the platform. Once there, my students dispersed, gone within minutes, leaving my family in Julia's capable hands.

It didn't surprise me when Julia brought us to this embodiment of a fairy-tale forest. She'd played the role of our fairy godmother perfectly up to that point. Spooky gray branches stretched out to our side. Specters loomed, dark under the taller limbs. They blocked all but the faintest glimmer of sunlight. The words of Goethe suddenly raced through my imagination: *Who rides so late through a night so wild? It is the father with his dear child.*

Every German schoolchild reads Goethe's poem, "Erlkönig," riding its galloping rhythm to its unthinkable end. The father only sees the trees and fog. But the son recognizes in these disguises the otherworldly king who will steal him away, leaving a dead body in the horrified father's arms.

The recognition washed over me, a fear of palpable, inevitable sorrow. It was still quite possible a similar scenario would play out with my program back home. And yet, recognizing this beloved poem in the landscape, reading in it a metaphor for my life, I also felt joy rise in me. Never before had this magic revealed itself so directly. We'd entered the world of Goethe, who spun the German language into literature while America fought to become a nation.

And—I see it now—this was the world of Jakob and Wilhelm Grimm, who followed on his heels. Not only did they collect fairy tales from women in places such as these, they also documented and organized the language that shaped those stories. And when Jakob wrote the rules down, he made the German language accessible. With those rules, he wove it together, intertwining all the Germans. And sweeping me up along with them. In this landscape, I was meeting my heroes.

This was the message I'd been expecting. But how should I interpret it? As a message of hope, that everything would be all right, or as an ironic nod to my beloved German program's impending last gasps? There was no way to know.

To our left, rocky terrain sloped sharply downward, and to the right, an equally steep carpet of underbrush rose up. I let my imagination carry us forward.

"Girls! We're like Red Riding Hood," I pointed toward cloaked shadows. "Do you think the wolf is watching?" I carried one daughter, then grasped her hand, then chased her on ahead. Likewise, Dave chased after the other. They half-heartedly joined in, wanting to believe, but not seeing as I did.

Julia stayed with us. The others had long since disappeared. We asked more questions to nudge our two weary girls onward.

"How fast can you run?" I asked. They ran for a moment.

"How many black beetles can you count in the needles?" I offered. They gave a cursory glance.

"How quickly do you think we can climb this mountain?" Dave tried. They dragged.

Julia paced herself, calmly observing our progress. At each twist and turn, every possible shortcut, we paused to consider. "If we take the wrong path," she said, "it will add hours to our hike."

We needed to get back before nightfall. My stomach rumbled. I thought of that restaurant at the base, of the hearty food we'd find there. My quadriceps and shoulders burned, but we continued. We cajoled the children forward, to save our own tired backs.

Finally, I look up and I see it: a tree branch frames the heavens. It's my favorite German romantic painting come to life, unfolding before us, blue sky breaking open. Like tiny people in that scene, we stand in the forefront, next to a split rail fence. On the other side, tree covered hills merge with fainter mounds rolling away. They disappear into eternity. My heart expands with the view. My shoulders release their burdens.

A carved pole crossed with two branches greets us, hung with brightly painted clay pots fashioned into bells. They chime *Willkommen*. Welcome home. It's taken you a lifetime, but you've arrived.

We stayed for a while, enjoyed glasses of *Weinschorle* and *Apfelschorle*—wine spritzer for the grownups, sparkling apple juice for the girls. We gazed upon the world, all-radiant in the sunshine, and scanned the hilltops for castle ruins.

Julia pointed. "That's the one where Richard the Lionhearted lived as a prisoner."

I hoped he had a window. Captivity with a view of this place suddenly sounded like heaven. Because if I could stay there, I wouldn't have to face the messes awaiting me back in America.

On our way out of town that morning, my daughters had spied a half-timbered building for sale. Looking over the landscape, they declared their intention to buy it. The castles had convinced them to stay.

"We'll open a bar and sell Apfelschorle," said Mira.

Olivia chimed in. "We can get a cuckoo clock with the money."

Far away, in a Minnesota school district, random administrators would take away my German classes someday, whether it was the next day or the next year. I would fight like hell until then, but part of me knew it was only a matter of time. They wouldn't let me out of their sights. And I would cease to be Frau Hallberg. When that time came, all the painful emotions would come crashing back to the fore. *At least I'll have a Spanish position*, I thought. The law ensured it.

But none of that mattered that day. Because I was Amy Hallberg, whose name means *Beloved Soundmountain*. And I belonged to this place. I knew this was true forevermore. A little piece of my soul lived there, will live there always, in the southwestern corner of Germany. And they could never take that away.

# 15

## Black Forest / Schwarzwald

Walking single file, the students boarded our bus in Strasbourg en route to the Schwarzwald. Josh stopped when he reached my seat and bent to look at me. He was wearing his usual black death metal T-shirt, and his wavy hair hung down over his eyes.

"May I please give a tour?" He sounded so sincere.

"What do you mean?"

"May I sit in the tour guide seat up front and lead the group on a tour?"

I considered his request. He'd spent two hours in France, exactly the same amount of time I had. After asking the driver's permission, I told him to go ahead.

Strasbourg is just across the Rhine from Baden-Württemberg. At various times among recent past wars, the city has been part of Germany. By 1987, it was solidly French; Americans needed visas for France, so Eva's parents never brought me. Now, nobody looked at our passports.

"Hello." Josh's sultry voice filled the bus. "I'm your tour guide, Josh. If you look to the right, you'll see a staircase to nowhere." I looked out the window and saw such a staircase. "This refers to the mysterious and seemingly purposeless nature of human existence." Seventeen Americans and their German hosts laughed with delight.

Josh struggled in German class and never completed his homework. After school I would find him climbing walls surrounding the building. When he'd asked to go on this trip, I insisted he come, even when his mother questioned my sanity. Maybe it was because I related to him— before I left for West Germany as a teen, my mom had told me point blank I couldn't handle Europe.

⌀

Our group ambled through rustic cabins, brought from all over and reassembled as one fictitious, timeworn village. Beside one fireplace, a lady wove at a loom. By another, a woman carved wooden whistles with birds on top. She blew one to demonstrate: *Coo-coo! Coo-coo!* It made the sound of a real cuckoo clock at a fraction of the price.

"Do you both want a whistle?" I asked Mira and Olivia. "She can burn your name on the side." I nearly held my breath until they agreed. I made sure they found the nicest birds.

Dave admired the two whistles and then turned to me. "Why don't you get yourself one? For your classroom."

I thought of my carefully crafted German microcosm and nodded, then chose a third whistle. We watched the lady burn *Frau H* into its side. By then, I'd decided to stand my sacred ground: I wasn't letting my program go without a fight.

After a lunch of bratwurst and spätzle, we ate our Black Forest cake. Geese paddled nearby in a stream. We stared at a pyramid farmhouse built into the hillside, the kind that shelters people and livestock beneath one enormous thatched roof.

I let myself savor every whimsical moment. Down the road, there was a giant toboggan track with coasters for us to ride down. I didn't even mind when we set out and Josh ran ahead, carrying Olivia on his back and holding Mira by the hand.

.☯

"The thing is," my longtime student Jenna said later, "your kids are adorable." She and four other girls in her room shoved clothing into bags. They emptied the same red gingham duvets and white pillow-cases they'd stuffed with bedding the previous night. We'd arrived at this Alpine lodge after dark, late for dinner. Now we were rushing to squeeze in a quick walk following breakfast.

Jenna piled linens outside their door. I noticed that sometime since leaving America, she'd dyed her usually bleached hair a rich chestnut brown.

She stood and rested her hands on her hips. "Just so you know, Frau, we've decided that when you're not around, I get Mira. Hannes and Josh get Olivia." Hannes was Josh's responsible host, whom I'd asked to check on the guys.

"Not today." I picked up my satchel. "I'm keeping my children with me."

I was on the edge of feeding my *Fernweh*—a yearning for a distant place that was never my home. We were moving on to Freiburg, the sunniest city in Germany, where cobblestone gullies would keep our feet dry even if it rained. For me in 1987, Freiburg was like its name, a fortress of freedom.

Back then, the stores stayed open only one Saturday afternoon a month. On those days, after morning classes, Mami and Papi would pick us up from school. As we drove into the Schwarzwald, Mami would pass Butterbröte mit Salami to Eva, Heiko, and me in the backseat. To wash it down, she'd hand us cans of Spezi—orange mixed with cola. During the hour-long trip, she fed scraps of sandwich and chocolate slivers to the dog curled up at her feet. Once we reached Freiburg, Eva and I would set off on our own, the clock ticking the minutes away. We never beat Mami and Papi back to the fountain where they waited, wiry ginger-haired dog on a short tether.

Twenty-two years later, I was still on a tight timeframe in Freiburg, and once again, somebody else was in charge. Julia and Sabina led our group to the cathedral steps and told us to return in two hours. Dave, Mira, and Olivia followed me through the pedestrian zone and patiently pretended to listen. I bought postcards. We ordered crêpes at a stand. I pointed out the bookstore where I bought my silver paperback copy of *Mephisto*, the book Eva had recommended so many years before. We picked out red T-shirts with kittens above the word *Freiburg*. Mira used her spending money to buy a Black Forest doll. It wore braided chestnut yarn hair, a black apron, and a red *Bollenhut*—a traditional hat for young ladies, covered in bright red pompoms.

We were eating ice cream cones at an outdoor café when a long-lost memory surfaced. "Look way up there—do you see the steeple?" I pointed to the Münster Cathedral. "We could climb the clock tower if we had time. You can see forever up there. When I was seventeen, I snuck away to Freiburg and went up there with a boy."

Dave feigned shock. "If you girls ever do that, you're grounded for life."

"Eva's parents were super protective. They didn't like this guy." I stared at the spire and let the details return. "And he was a jerk. That belfry is super high, and I was terrified. He ran down ahead on the spiral staircase and kept reaching around to grab my ankle."

I had their attention. Olivia stared wide-eyed. Mira leaned in. "What did you do?"

"I screamed at him to stop, and then he bought me ice cream."

Dave chortled and grabbed some napkins to wipe the girls' faces. "Don't take dating advice from your mother."

To tell the truth, I'd known better when it came to Thomas, the first boy to talk to me in Germany and the first anywhere to look at me with hunger in his eyes. From the day we first met, his affections ran hot and cold. His mixed-message notes, delivered by friends, centered on his love of America. However, at nineteen, he'd had something I wanted that sixteen-year-old Eva did not: a driver's license. He also represented a potential future.

A couple of weeks before my first trip to Germany ended, our farewell looming, I saw my best shot at life in the Schwarzwald slipping away. Thomas sped along twisted backroads driving me home, and I made my final plea, direct as I dared: I could study in Freiburg.

He kept his eyes on the road and said it would never work. He dropped me off at home before sunset, but not before he'd extracted an invitation to visit me in Minnesota, which led to a curious postscript: when Thomas showed up at my house two months later, I rejected him in the same way he'd turned me down. It wasn't a relationship we wanted. The culprit was that *Fernweh*—a longing not for each other, but for the love of a distant land.

℘

Once again, I didn't want to leave Freiburg. We walked to our prearranged meeting spot on the cathedral steps. We hid from the sun in the archway. I handed Olivia and Mira fruit from the market, a brown paper bag of cherries and another of plums. The juice dribbled down their fingers, and Dave dabbed their hands again. This was what I wanted all along: to stand in the Freiburger Marktplatz with my American husband and our sweet American twins.

"I love Freiburg," I said to Josh, who found Dave and me on the steps. Josh looked like he very much wanted to join my daughters, climbing along the too-small ledge beneath medieval stone-carved apostles. I felt on edge. "I never get enough time in Freiburg."

Josh nodded. "This guy in the street let me play his harmonica. It was awesome."

I chuckled. "You didn't. What will I tell your mom?"

More teenagers gathered nearby. Several wore the bright blue T-shirt I designed, the Karlsruhe castle topped by our school logo, a bird. In the foreground I'd drawn an iconic Minneapolis fountain: a giant cherry on an enormous spoon. All these disparate pieces somehow made sense.

On the back was a Beethoven quote, in English, discovered by one of my students: "Never shall I forget the time I spent with you. Please continue to be my friend, as you will always find me yours."

*❧*

It had dawned on me what I was doing this time around. I was coming to terms with my past. Germans have a word for this: *Vergangenheitsbewältigung*. It shares a root with *Gewalt*—meaning violence. What led us into dark places, and how did we find our way through?

When I was seventeen in the backseat of Mami and Papi's car, the road from Donaueschingen brought us through the Höllental, or Valley of Hell. As we approached the spot, Eva would watch out the window and at the right moment cry, "Amy, look up!" At that moment, I would crane my neck to catch a glimpse of the *Hirschsprung*, meaning "stag's leap."

The bronze statue stood on a cliff above the road, riddled with bullets from multiple wars, but magnificent all the same. According to legend, a stag once escaped from hunters there by jumping across the gorge. My pulse raced to see it, a beacon reminding us we would emerge from the forest, safe on the other side.

Twenty-two years later, driving into Freiburg, we bypassed the Hirschsprung for good reason: there's no direct path through the Schwarzwald. You can choose between scenic routes, or you can aim for relative speed.

Until Julia laid out our options that morning, I hadn't thought of the statue in years. The bus driver took another road, and we gained half an hour in Freiburg. On the road back to Karlsruhe, for the life of me, I couldn't get the Hirschsprung out of my head. I pictured the space between cliffs—one single moment of grace. And I wondered, what was the truth behind that immortalized leap—and every German story I tell?

When they were children, Eva's parents had been forced to take that kind of leap. Now it was creeping up on me, this incredible guilt. Thanks to their kindness, I walked so easily through this German world.

❧

One week later, Eva and her parents were waiting once again, and I couldn't catch my breath. She'd emailed a photo of four beds made up with blankets for our daughters' slumber party. At last they were sleeping under one roof. Not the rental twin house where I first stayed, but the dream home Mami and Papi built on the edge of the Schwarzwald. Dave and I would sleep in Donaueschingen's best hotel that night, a stone's throw away from the prior weekend's lodge.

First thing that morning, we had barreled south on the Autobahn. Dave rode shotgun; I drove in a vain attempt to calm my nerves. Painful tension ran the length of my arms. I tried—and failed—to shake them loose. My heart pounded against the walls of my chest when I reached the right exit.

♫

From years of teaching *The White Rose*, I knew Hans and Sophie Scholl grew up wandering those low-lying mountains—the Swabian Alps. Near here they learned the love of country that called them to the end of their lives, along with their love of books and their Lutheran faith.

When I taught the Scholls' story, I set the stage by showing *Triumph des Willens*. Students would say the Hitler Youth in action reminded them of Boy Scouts; they were shocked to admit the activities looked like great fun. And every time we watched it, I searched for Hans's face, because he was at that rally. The Hitler Youth was mandatory—he may well have been one of those nameless boys, speaking in memorized call and response. Somehow he and Sophie turned out differently from other youths of their generation.

Mami and Papi grew up in that world. Their generosity floors me to this day. As an American teen in the eighties, I had no idea what it meant for them to watch over me. They fed me good food. They drove me to church on Sundays. As a grownup, I understood how many clues I had missed.

To my knowledge, Mami had never returned to the Prussian hometown she knew as Königsberg. I didn't know Papi's war story. I did know they gave me the idyllic German childhood they'd never had.

$\mathcal{C}$

When their neighborhood came into view, I immediately recognized the white Alpine house with the red tile roof. It felt almost shameless to ask them for more, especially arriving late again. I parked on the road and plastered a smile on my face. We knocked at the kitchen door and it opened. Mami appeared there, hair whiter than ever.

"*Nun seid ihr wieder da!*" she exclaimed. "*Kommt mal rein.*"—You're back! Come on in! She gave me a hug, shook Dave's hand, and admired my twins. Eva came in and set down some dishes to give us all hugs. Her young son trailed her closely. Two daughters scrambled into the room: spirited, miniature versions of Eva.

It was all I needed to relax and catch my breath.

The four girls squealed and ran off before we could introduce them. Their voices echoed up and down the stairs. Papi led us into the dining room. Eva carried in plates of cold cuts and cheeses, breads and jellies, tomatoes, cucumber, and melon. She poured fizzy water and sparkling black tea, then called our collective children to the table.

"We're the chaos team!" said Eva's eldest, Carlotta. Her sister, Sophia, and my girls followed, all squeezing in together. Their laughter punctuated our meal.

Mami tried to coax her oldest granddaughter to eat, as she once more successfully coaxed me. Eva shook her head, loving but stern. "*Mama! Die sind Kinder.*" Meaning, remember they're kids. They'll eat what they want.

After our adventures in town, Eva suggested a walk in the woods. Sunlight streamed through the branches, making little diamonds of light on the ground. It was a beautiful day, topped off by a meal of roast pork, potatoes, and salad that Papi prepared himself. Afterward, he and his grandson retreated to the cellar. He'd built a miniature village that filled a whole room, surrounded by model trains that whistled as they made their rounds.

Dave and I drove away at dusk, following Eva's taillights to our hotel. At the lobby bar we ordered three glasses of wine—white for me, red for Eva and Dave.

"Do you think the girls will sleep tonight?" I asked, happy for the moment of calm.

Dave laughed aloud. Eva raised her eyebrows. "They will be up for hours," she said. "I'll go back soon to rescue my poor parents."

I thought of the room upstairs with four giggling girls and their beds draped in white blankets. I pictured Mira curled up with the Black Forest doll she chose for herself.

And I smiled. Once again, Eva and I had found a way to bridge our two worlds.

# PART THREE

# Weiterleben / Living On

2009—2012

# 16

## Divided Loyalties / Geteilte Loyalität

By the grace of God and administrators, I returned from that fairytale trip of 2009 to a newly reconfigured German position. As of September, I'd spend mornings at my current building—now renamed West High School—and afternoons in the brand new high school a couple miles to the east. And I was simply grateful I'd held onto my program, albeit in diminished form.

Once upon a (very recent) time, I'd told my students without a hint of irony that teaching them was my dream job. Facilitating small groups, playing with grammar and words, sitting together in circles, unpacking stories and poems—I loved all of that.

I especially adored bringing the language to life with German films. I stumbled onto *The Harmonists* six months before I met Dave in 1999. Before then, I'd never heard of the Comedian Harmonists, a sensation virtually forgotten since the Weimar Republic. A brilliant German singing group with an American-sounding name, they appeared destined for lasting fame. In retrospect, they were doomed from the start.

In my ten years of showing the film, I'd developed a whole routine. I will long remember the last group I introduced to the Harmonists in

March 2009, raucous boys who volleyed German back and forth at top volume and girls who ignored them as much as possible.

"*Achtung*," I said, my reminder to be careful, as I ushered them into our state-of-the-art digital language lab.

"*Ja wohl!*" the boys responded en masse. They sounded militaristic and mean. Maybe I did too, but I'd taken the lead on securing this precious space.

As usual when I played the first song, my crew looked at the black-and-white picture of the group in our textbook: six tuxedoed men, one wearing a monocle. Predictably, muted groans arose. I asked them to listen and write down words they heard. I couldn't read their blank expressions. I steeled myself for this, trusting I would soon win them over.

"OK," I said in conclusion. "What do you think?"

"It's so outdated," a curly-haired boy in the back row called out. His buddies nodded, and murmurs broke out.

"The words or the music?" I asked. "Both," came the predictable response. But I held out hope. In the days that followed, we watched the film, scene by scene. I led them in digesting it slowly, one ninety-minute class at a time. I saw how students leaned forward, enchanted by five singers and their accompanist on a grand piano, together commanding center stage.

The Comedian Harmonists' namesake comedic wordplay and masterful harmonies drew fans just as reliably during their Weimar heyday. Not at the end of Weimar Germany, when a splintered electorate gave rise to the Third Reich. And not in that infamous period of economic free fall in the immediate aftermath of World War I, when chaos and anarchy threatened to subsume any government in Berlin. It happened in that in-between space, a small window when visionary legislators assembled at the National Theater in out-of-the-way Weimar to establish a progressive German government.

In that brief, improbable moment, the Harmonists succeeded in Berlin beyond their wildest dreams. Their records flew off the shelves. They consistently filled concert halls, perhaps the most famous singing ensemble in Europe. They had it all: friendship and love and fame and fortune. They balanced innuendo-laden songs with tender, romantic *Lieder*. They performed for Nazi officials, who extended invitations and silenced Brownshirts chanting, "*Juden raus!*" at the back of balconies. Later, US Navy sailors hosted them on a ship.

All this was Harry Frommerman's brainchild, to emulate the American musical spirit. A bassist named Bob Biberti helped him bring the group to life. And I could relate to that. Because I, too, had poured my heart into building community around foreign passions.

Within days of starting the film that last time, the curly-haired boy breezed into my classroom. "Frau," he said, waving his smartphone. "Check it out. I downloaded the soundtrack." He huddled with his buddies around a desk, each singing snippets of harmony. I felt a rush of pride run through me.

By then, storm clouds were gathering onscreen. The Comedian Harmonists weren't fated to live happily ever after. Relationships wore thin. At the peak of success, they were banned from performing. Half of the members were Jewish and needed to leave the country. Even knowing what was coming, we couldn't bear to look away.

The Comedian Harmonists gave a final concert in Munich. By the day those scenes rolled in class, everyone joined in, all of us singing from memory:

*Gib mir ein letztes Abschiedskuss*

*Weil ich dich heut' verlassen muss*

*Und sage mir Auf Wiedersehen.*

*Auf Wiedersehen. Leb wohl.*

Like the audience, shocked and entranced, we knew what those words meant:

Give me one last farewell kiss. Because today I must leave.

And say to me *Auf Wiedersehen. Auf Wiedersehen,* live well.

*Auf Wiedersehen.* Until we see each other again.

Agility in German was the Comedian Harmonists' strong suit, their connection to the world. The group sang together as long as they could. And then they said goodbye.

Goodbye to the Comedian Harmonists. And goodbye to the way things had been. We watched the ensemble go their separate ways on a crowded station platform, singers waving out the window as the train pulled away, never to set eyes on each other again. Despite their American-sounding name, the three Jewish exiles never made it big as the Comedy Harmonists; German was out of fashion in America by then. Nor did the Christians' reconfigured, renamed Meistersextett recapture their previous glory in Germany.

I read the film as a cautionary tale, even before my near-transfer to middle school Spanish. Change was already on the horizon in my district, in the name of school reform, following a wave of new leadership hires in recent years.

It turned out all bets were off once this new administration came into its own.

I first saw East High School the day after we wrapped up *The Harmonists* that last time in March, on my way to a meeting to explore scheduling options. Administrators had asked for teacher input. Waiting at a red light, I studied the emerging fortress, its sheets of glass façade rising above wetlands, the sky beyond it framing a white weather ball atop a steel tower.

Just then, a semi cab caught my eye as it rounded the corner too quickly. Watching from my minivan, I saw the accident in my mind's eye a moment before it happened.

The empty flatbed swung out onto the icy road, slamming into several cars immediately ahead of me. The flatbed swept away, then planed back to plow into a car directly behind me. The vehicles spun out of place, careening, crunching, coming to rest all around, never touching my motionless car.

Mercifully, no one appeared to be injured, though everyone was visibly shaken. Because my car wasn't damaged, the police told me to go on my way. I willed myself to believe it was a sign: everything would turn out all right.

I arrived at the meeting early, open to possibilities, ready to share my love of teaching in ninety-minute blocks. Having time to fully immerse ourselves made me a better teacher. My students overwhelmingly agreed.

"This isn't about you," said a man I knew well. "This is about what's best for students."

A high-ranking woman I'd never met said, "Students only like the block schedule because it's easier for them."

In the end, school district leaders announced a complex hybrid system: short classes of forty-nine minutes some days, ninety-minute blocks on others, high class sizes to offset costs for the most expensive staffing option. Also, we were adding ninth grade. Taking a group to Germany would prove nothing compared with navigating my whirlwind schedule.

Come September, after East High School opened, that same intersection out front—now divided by concrete—would become one of few places where I could stop and breathe.

Not everything changed. My top students still read fairy tales and Goethe's poems. I still showed films to illustrate Germany's modern descent into darkness and the long climb out. It's just that I wasn't present. Because in addition to traveling over my prep time, I taught two levels of German at once, three out of five classes. It was the only way administrators could figure out how to offer all those half-filled levels from a divided student body.

In January, several master teachers chose to take early retirement. That wasn't an option for me, so I kept going. I scarfed my cafeteria lunches after I finished teaching at West. I digested my morning's events waiting for 2.6 miles' worth of stoplights to change. Heavy laden, I walked from visitor parking through the East High lunchroom to a deserted hallway. Multiple keys hung from a lanyard around my neck, along with my ID and a tiny schedule to keep me on track. I was never ready to teach when forty-plus students arrived.

Rushing between the desks in the classroom, making my way up front, I would finish scrawling basic verb charts across the whiteboard, then head for the door, calling out final instructions to absolute beginners, seated in groups of three and four. "Frau! Frau!" they called in response. But I had to get to the lounge, where my more advanced classes waited.

Students from both groups often stepped in my path—"*Frau!*"—but I waved them away. "I've told you what to do. Read the board." It's hardly defensible; it was what I could do. In the remaining minutes, I toted a portable whiteboard and dying markers to the lounge outside.

Closing the door, I'd call out in German, "Join me with your copies of Kafka."

Students scrambled from every corner, carrying benches, jockeying for the sofa, leaving the center space open for me. The rest circled us on the carpet. I breathed while they found the right page, then dove in. "Gregor Samsa awoke one day after restless dreams and discovered himself transformed into a giant vermin." They stared at their books, blank expressions giving way while I spoke. "Look at this phrase. '*Flimmernde Beine.*' Say it with me."

"Flim-mairn-da By-na," said the voices in chorus.

"Those are his flimsy, useless legs waving above his head. And his *panzerartiges Rücken*," I continued. "Stuck in bed on his back like a tank." I leaned back and waved my arms. "Can't you just see him lying there, helpless?"

Spoiler alert: I suspected I was that oversized vermin, possibly a dung beetle, flailing at the onset of a lingering, inevitable demise. There was no longer sweetness in my voice when speaking to students, hardly any for my own children either. I heard persistent whispers of sun-setting

German. If not enough students signed up in the future, German would cease to be offered, first level one, then two. And finally my beloved literature classes would disappear.

Given that context, it was an enormous problem that I hadn't found my rhythm, especially at East. Seven minutes after the bell, additional students straggled in, fresh off the bus from West. Those same students rose to leave at the warning bell, seven minutes early. While I frantically wrapped things up, the bell often startled me midsentence. Students scattered. A few times, I grabbed my forehead with both hands and howled. And then two more parallel groups would start drifting in.

By 3:00 p.m., I'd make a long-delayed trip to the restroom. The mirror reflected silver strands multiplying daily, though I'd just passed my fortieth birthday. I noted the unpleasant sensation of my hair perpetually standing on end.

On good days, I didn't have to tutor students at West before picking my daughters up from after-school care. Settling behind my East desk, I could take several breaths and knead my shoulders, then dig into work: respond to emails, send forgotten attendance, plan the next day's lessons, attend to mounting pile of papers, enter a backlog of grades.

I stayed seated at my desk until the sky glowed red. I frequently stopped and gazed out the window at the darkening hills, the view undeniably reminiscent of Germany.

One singular goal spurred me on: *I will stay in this room until I turn this mess around.*

⌇

The first genuine hint of trouble had arrived in February 2008. My then principal came to inform me I'd been denied a position on a key committee. This had never happened in my history with the district; I'd been actively recruited. I couldn't help crying with him still standing there, pulling myself together by explaining why it was OK. He listened before awkwardly slipping away. That Sunday—a gorgeous, snowy afternoon—a miracle happened. A stranger called my cell phone and mentioned the name of my parents' Lutheran church.

"Your dad tells me you sang 'O Holy Night' on Christmas Eve."

"Yes?" This felt important.

"I direct a community choir," he said. "Would you have time to come over? I'd like to hear you sing." He was rehearsing Mozart's Requiem, which I sang in college. On the side, he was staging a cabaret. Dave and the girls insisted I go. That's how I found myself basking in the adoring glow of a spotlight, singing my vintage torch song on Valentine's Day.

As fortune would have it, another soprano had recently joined the choir—a gorgeous blond, fifteen years younger, with the perfect voice to complement mine. At the director's request, we choreographed a full-body catfight, each wearing furry ears and a tail sewed by Mom. Our classical aria consisted of meows. This spared us the trouble of lyrics.

Afterward Mira clasped her arms around my legs, eyes wide with excitement. "She didn't really hurt you!"

"You were so wonderful, Mommy," Olivia said. The praises of my children warmed my heart. But I sang for myself.

Eventually, I grew disillusioned. The director told me he never wanted to lead a choir without my voice in it. He refused to let me sing in ensembles with partners I chose. He said my voice was too precious to waste. After all my time chasing solos, I should've felt honored. Instead, I felt constrained and pressed to memorize music. Eventually I quit.

*✧*

Given this history, it made no sense that in September 2009, right when East High School opened, I joined the exacting choir at our downtown Minneapolis church. Every Wednesday, Dave retrieved the girls while I braved the worst of rush hour traffic, grabbing dinner in the church basement.

I discovered the choir's true appeal during my first rehearsal. Someone asked the proper pronunciation of the German letters "ch."

Always the expert, I leapt to my feet. "It's the sound a cat makes when it hisses."

My fellow singers glanced over, then shifted their gazes to the renowned professional soloist two chairs to my right. I sat down. She rose, poised and angelic, to demonstrate the sound. My cheeks burned, and I let my thoughts drift. Soon I settled into the feeling. And I understood why I would remain: I would never be asked to lead, nor stand center-stage as I did on demand every day. I could lose myself in magnificent harmonies, knowing we'd sound good, never having to go off script. We sang inspired anthems and moved on. One set for early November washed across my brain for weeks—*We are born, we live, and we fade away.*

The Sunday we sang that anthem, I started to cry, with good reason. My aunt Vivian would pass on later that week, following a devastating struggle with Alzheimer's. We hadn't said goodbye in person. I smelt her perfume that morning while walking past my garbage can. It was a strange sensation to mourn the aunt I'd been missing, who was already gone, to pray for her release while longing to hear her voice. She'd have known what to say about this mess. She was the first person who taught me how to interpret signs. Vivian would have offered the title of a soul-soothing book. She definitely would have gotten my Kafka reference.

Sitting at that East desk before parent-teacher conferences, I received the email confirmation I'd been expecting from my cousin. I felt the lump in my throat and silent, heaving gasps in my chest. White clouds draped the hills outside. I looked up to see two parents standing in the door and froze. I couldn't place them. Bear in mind, I invited them myself.

"I'm sorry," I stammered. "My favorite aunt died."

"Oh, Amy," said the mother. "We can reschedule."

"No." I wiped my eyes. "You're here. Come on in." There were plenty more parents coming, all of whom I needed as partners if this German program was to survive.

I couldn't possibly take time off. Ben traveled to meet Mom for the funeral. I poured my love into a eulogy and sent it for my cousin to read at the service. Aunt Vivian gave me so many stories to draw on, from years of candid phone conversations.

"You can say anything you like, if you say it sweetly enough." Her words would drip with honey as she spoke. "You can say 'shit' right to someone's face."

After my aunt's passing, I felt her presence everywhere: the heaviness she carried within her tiny frame, and her abundant laughter. When one dream played itself out, my aunt gave herself permission to dream another. I started cobbling together a second exchange trip. Every time I looked out over the mist-shrouded hill, I remembered: *Mist means shit in German.*

I seemed to have landed in it, a joke my aunt would've liked.

In late August and September 2010, when the following school year began, I was spending every weekend at the local Renaissance Festival, dressed as a peasant. "Soup, glorious soup!" I sang out. At the stand across the way, Dave wore similar garb, hawking Sprite, which he dubbed "pixies in a cup." Along with students and families, we were fundraising for our upcoming trip. Thank God, I had a parent on board to manage schedules for our two venues.

"When are you coming home?" our children asked each time we left them with Mom, knowing we'd both have grading when we returned and no energy to parent.

Ramping up my insane schedule of the year before, administrators assigned me an hour of Spanish One at West High. (Remember, I'd never taught Spanish.) It came right after a combination of German Two and German Three, plus twenty devoted students teaching themselves AP German in a nearby modular classroom. Sadly, that part was my doing. I'd convinced administrators to let me make this Faustian bargain, because I'd set a precedent, and students begged to continue. Otherwise, we wouldn't have advanced German.

Julia and Sabine arrived two months into this landscape with a fresh group of teens, divided between two schools. From their first day, Julia's West crew joined my top learners in their makeshift classroom. Whenever I peeked in, they all called out "*Spitze*," meaning a high point. They joined their fingertips, pointed upward like the peak of a mountain. "*Absolut Spitze*," they repeated—absolutely the summit.

Over at East, I arrived to find several gangly boys sitting with Sabine in the lounge. "Aa-my!" she called in ringing tones. "The lunch schedule isn't right."

I sighed and put down my bags outside my locked door. She handed me her paperwork. Since I never taught classes at lunchtime, I had no clue how I'd gone wrong.

I'd taken a day off from school to arrange those schedules. There were lunch codes that corresponded with money already deposited by host families. It was hugely complicated, and I'd felt so proud of myself.

"Just have them eat whenever," I finally said.

At my house that evening, Julia and Sabine brought up lunches again. "I read the schedule wrong," I said. "Can't they sort out plans with their partners?"

Julia and Sabine exchanged glances, tipping their heads in that stoic German way. "Why can't you sort it out?" Julia said at last.

I had no answer. Countless times during those two school years, I'd awoken at three in the morning with a fragment of an idea. I'd run to my office and typed up a worksheet to get through the following day. I spent additional sleepless nights on a daybed in the girls' playroom, watching the moon wax and wane while Dave slept in our bed. My heart gripped my chest, and tension crawled up my arms.

And that was before their group's arrival.

They had each other and the backing of their school. I had permission to let them show up, nothing more. In the coming weeks, I'd watch them through my classroom window, loading their students onto buses for excursions I arranged. I wondered how this would end.

$\mathcal{O}$

After they sorted out lunch, the "East Germans," as they jokingly called themselves, began ditching classes at will, dropping into my room and camping out with students in the lounge. Much to my relief, Americans from both high schools and their German partners made arrangements for socializing outside of school. They drove each other all over town for backyard bonfires. They even held a volleyball tournament in the East Gym and dubbed it their "International Olympics."

The morning the Germans left for the airport, I gathered with the East students and their partners on steps inside the door to take pictures. The group raised their hands in jubilant peaks. "*Spitze*," they called out. Then they meandered out into the parking lot by the wetlands. When the bus arrived from West, Germans fresh from saying goodbye across town filed out to hug their East friends, too. Finally, I chased all the reunited Germans onto the bus. Once inside, they stuck their hands out the windows. The Americans formed a procession, slapping each hand, tears streaming down their faces as the bus pulled away.

I returned to my classroom, feeling an expansiveness in my heart. I'd kept my German program and the exchange alive. Still, happily ever after is the American fairy tale ending.

The Grimms' version says this: *And they lived and they lived, and if they're not dead, then they're living on still.* I had to ask myself: what was the point of continuing on after you've lived past your dreams?

# 17

## Classical Weimar / Weimar Klassizismus

It was only a matter of time before I started painting again.

After we moved into our house in 2006, I'd painted and repainted our great room in various shades of white. I knew too well the panic that drove me to sneak off and buy just one more gallon of the most expensive paint. Dave would come down to the main level in the morning, see me up on a ladder surrounded by plastic drop cloths, and retreat into the basement without saying a word. Olivia and Mira, at age three . . . and four . . . and five, cajoled me before giving up. My creative spirit demanded expression.

Finally, to cover the glaring flaws where afternoon light streamed through, Mom wallpapered our front entry. She was exhausted from listening to my obsession with color. For a few years, that and choir settled my impulse.

And then in March 2010, three months before our second trip to Karlsruhe, Olivia announced she needed her own room. Mira agreed. I'd been hoping to wait until they were teens. But at age seven, they bickered constantly every morning, making it nearly impossible to get out the door on time. I made time for the move. Even though we were overbooked, even though Dave resisted because he had papers to grade every weekend, I needed sanity. My parents agreed to help. Mira kept the original room while Olivia got my tiny office next door.

In exchange, I claimed their spacious Peony Pink playroom as my writer's studio, plus its Drop Dead Gorgeous Red walk-in closet, dubbed by the girls "the secret room." The fighting diminished. My painting resumed.

I coated my walls in multiple pinks before stumbling onto a serene blue I could live with. A few weeks before school ended, I painted the secret room versions of green. Finally, my decorator friend, Christi from choir, scheduled a house call intervention.

"Okay, girl." She slipped off her heels on her way in and headed up the staircase. "Show me what's going on."

Inside my studio, Christi set down her paint swatches case and looked around. I held my breath. She stopped at the closet, freshly re-surfaced with Seedling Green. She ran her fingers through strawberry blond hair, pulled back into a ponytail. "I don't see the problem," she finally proclaimed. "This green is perfect. However . . ." she gestured toward the dark beige hallway. "Let's move some things around here."

For half an hour, she cheerfully hammered nails into walls, reposi-tioned framed prints, and directed me to buy some mirrors and a few baskets to bring the space to life. "Now." She set the hammer on a book-shelf. "This beige isn't you. What will make you happy?" She flipped through a book of swatches and deftly plucked out a mossy green square. She held it by the wall. "This one."

I picked up another stack. "How about . . ."

"That's how you got into trouble, remember?" She took the book from my hands and gave me the paper. Her blue eyes twinkled. "When you have time, paint the hallway this color. Then stop." She started packing up. "This green will make you happy."

I made time as soon as school ended. I had trouble focusing on other commitments. Like packing for Germany. Or writing. Or being a mom.

❧

A week after school got out and one week before we left home, Dave found our daughters in the backyard, cradling baby birds from a nest. He made the girls return them. Later Olivia came upon the babies, dead in the grass, and Dave helped bury them. He waited until that evening to tell me. "She knows she caused it." He looked so sad. "I tried to reassure her."

Olivia never mentioned it to me. I was surely too busy in my studio, sorting piles of paperwork. Possibly touching up paint.

On the morning our second group flew to Frankfurt—a Tuesday—my family arrived late at the Minneapolis–St. Paul airport to find every one of my students and all their parents waiting. Of course I blamed my daughters, but it was my fault. I stayed too long in my writer's studio, staring at its serene blue walls.

❧

The four of us had barely set down our suitcases in Julia's entryway when she said, "You should drive to Weimar, where Goethe and Schiller lived." She handed Dave two guidebooks from her bookshelf and showed me a keychain, a pressed gingko leaf from a recent road trip with her daughter. "Goethe loved gingko trees."

Reading over Dave's shoulder, my eyes landed on a reference to Goethe's first book, *The Sorrows of Young Werther*. I gasped. "The Duke invited Goethe to live in Weimar because of *Werther*?"

For years I'd mocked the melodrama of the sappy English translation I read in college. If they stayed with me long enough, my students all heard the backstory: Goethe was a law student who aspired to write. Suffering over a failed romance, unhappy in his career, he wrote his novella at twenty-four to purge the pain, killing his protagonist rather than himself. The book tapped into the *Zeitgeist*—the spirit of the time. After its publication, the book sparked a wave of suicides across Germany. Passionate young men shot themselves, dressed in blue jackets and yellow cravats, the same as Werther at his death.

"*Werther* made Goethe a celebrity," Julia said. She grabbed the guidebook and flipped to a picture of Goethe's walled-in garden. "The Duke gave Goethe two houses and made him a trusted advisor."

As it so happened, I knew this. I'd recently received a large envelope from Eva, immediately recognizable by her jaunty script. Two postcards inside pictured Goethe's desks in Weimar: one in the city, one on the outskirts of town. A magnet with Goethe's handwriting proclaimed, "*Lieben belebt*"—Love actively. A verb. Or "loves alive," a plural noun. I couldn't decide. Julia's synchronicity couldn't be mere coincidence.

Dave glanced from me to the page. I saw us in Goethe's garden, sitting under Goethe's gingko tree.

Julia pulled up a website and scrolled through images of rooms to rent. "The students will be occupied next weekend," she said. "You'll be back in Baden-Württemberg in a day."

$\mathscr{D}$

We set out Friday morning, pulling into Weimar by late afternoon. We had tight shoulders, numbed minds, and just enough time to walk into town for a tour of Goethe's home.

"I don't see a house," Dave said when we found the address.

"It's hot," Olivia whined. "I want ice cream."

I stared at the map. "It's got to be here." We'd barely needed it until that moment.

Finally we spotted a plaque by an unassuming door in a yellow wall. A few young men on the steps moved aside, and we entered through the gift shop. That's where I saw the extensive displays of gingko and painted color wheels. And Goethe had my attention.

From books on one table, I figured out that modern color theory—including complimentary colors—originated with Goethe's work as a scientist and artist. His handwritten captions labeled yellow good, green useful, blue common, indigo unnecessary, fuchsia beautiful, orange noble. I agreed that colors affect us, mind, body, and spirit. I disagreed about indigo.

Dave perked up at the threshold of Goethe's personal quarters. He took one look at the Latin greeting—*Salve,* black letters inlaid across honeyed wood—and said with a satisfied grin, "Goethe is one of my people." That was enough to win over the girls.

We wandered from room to room, where the walls matched paint colors throughout my house. In the room where illustrious guests once mingled, I saw the serene blue of my writing space. Goethe's books and classical treasures resided in rooms painted mossy and seedling greens.

At the doorway to his bedroom, I pondered the chair where my hero died at 89, adjacent to the room where he often wrote until after midnight. I heard Dave whisper in Mira's ear, "Mommy would love a writing space attached to her bedroom."

"Mommy would love most of Goethe's life," I replied.

The only thing missing was the gingko trees. We wandered blissful around his garden, posing and snapping tons of pictures. But we didn't see any telltale fan-shaped leaves. So we decided to hunt for gingko the next day, after we visited Schiller's house.

*⁊*

My family sat on a bench, eating our breakfast of *Brötchen* and *Wurst*—bakery rolls topped with cold cuts from a Weimar butcher. Goethe and Schiller stood before us in the plaza, green-tinged bronzes holding a laurel wreath, their hands clasped in friendship. Schoolchildren scrambled at their feet.

Sunlight gleamed from the Schiller department store rooftop. On the Nationaltheater, a bright blue banner announced their production of Goethe's *Die Wahlverwandtschaften*—known in unwieldy English as *Elective Affinities*. In it, Goethe makes his case that we are inexplicably drawn to those people whose energy changes the core of our being.

"The statue with Schiller was Goethe's idea," I read from the guidebook.

"How about the green wine bottle wedged between them?" Dave asked.

I smirked. "Let's get some pictures." The girls leapt up, predictably eager to pose beside German landmarks.

For a decade, Goethe and Schiller collaborated with such synergy that together, they launched a literary movement: German—or Weimar—Classicism. The only thing missing from this scene was Schiller's world-famous poem *An die Freude*, set to passionate music in Beethoven's Ninth Symphony.

Few Americans know Schiller's name, but almost everyone

recognizes "Ode to Joy." I've taught the poem ever since, side by side with Goethe's works.

*Deine Zauber binden wieder, was die Mode streng geteilt.*

*Alle Menschen werden Brüder wo dein sanfter Flügel weilt.*

Your magic binds together that which fashion forces apart.

All people become brothers where your gentle wings abide.

When they first met, Schiller found Goethe arrogant, and Goethe dismissed Schiller out of hand. After several years of acquaintance, Schiller wrote Goethe a letter proposing they form a friendship. Their now-inseparable presence permeates modern Weimar.

Something about my friendship with Eva has always surprised me in that same way. At sixteen, I didn't recognize my longed-for sister in her application picture. But when her first letter arrived in a colored envelope with cut-and paste letters spelling my name, I knew our pairing was meant to be.

✑

A display of busts greeted us inside the gift shop door: several life-sized Schillers beside two bins of cookie cutters—Goethe and Schiller in profile.

To this day, a life-sized ceramic bust of Schiller lurks among the student body of Carleton College, my Minnesota alma mater. It was originally stolen from a college president, and now Schiller's stealthy guardians show up at events and yell, "Schillerrrrrrrrr!" They run across the space, holding his bust aloft. If you move fast, you can steal him away.

Over the years, people have tussled over our Schiller and broken him, leaving competitors to struggle over fragments. A few times the college has collected the pieces and commissioned someone to buy an official replacement in Weimar.

"Do you want your own bust of Schiller?" Dave deadpanned.

I shook my head. "It costs a hundred euros."

We moved on to the Schiller Museum, barely a house anymore. Red block lettering on a spare white wall grabbed my attention. "*Die Räuber kosteten mir Familie und Vaterland*," I read aloud—*The Robbers* cost me family and fatherland. In other words, everything. Seeking an explanation, I scanned a large poster, an accounting of Schiller's life superimposed on a reproduction painting of the Thüringen landscape. And there was my answer: *The Robbers* was Schiller's first play. I only remembered *Wilhelm Tell*.

"Listen to this," I said to my family. "Schiller ran away from home. He came from near Stuttgart, like we did yesterday."

"How come he left?" Mira said.

"He deserted his post as a military doctor to attend his play's premiere. The Duke of Württemberg ordered him to stop writing."

"But that's not fair," Olivia said. "How could the Duke say that?"

"He was in charge. And this was a separate land." I pointed to the poster. "See? No bridges over the valleys."

"Or tunnels through mountains," Dave added.

They wandered off while I pored over Schiller's timeline: Starting over from scratch. Sickness that dogged him. Teaching at the University of Jena for free-will student offerings. Cultivating friendships. Supporting his wife and children. Constantly writing. Forging a literary movement with Goethe. All before Schiller's death in 1805.

I looked for his birth, found 1759, did the math, arrived at forty-five. I shivered in the climate-controlled room. I must've known all this once.

Afterward, I found Dave in a room off the stairwell. Mira and Olivia sat perched at tables, each with her own inkpot and quill. A woman in a green apron hung papers to dry. She smiled and nodded permission. Dave continued upstairs with me. In the same room with his writing desk, adorned with the writer's tools of his day, lies the bed where Schiller died at forty-five.

Forty-five.

*Forty-five.*

When I learned that fact at twenty-two, it must've sounded old. Now that I was forty-one, not so much.

Back in the quill room, the girls wrote on. "How did he die?" I asked the woman watching them.

"Lung disease," she said. "Tuberculosis." She handed me several pieces of paper. I flipped through pages inked with my daughters' names.

"And how did his family survive?" I asked.

"They stayed on in Weimar. Received money from local nobility, Goethe probably. And his widow composed verses to sell."

That day, I decided I could justify twenty-nine euros for my downsized bust of Schiller. He'd fit perfectly in my luggage, along with my poster of Goethe's painted walls and Dave's welcome mat imitation of Goethe's classical threshold.

☙

After leaving Schiller's house, we followed a trail of landmarks to Goethe's garden home. The park surrounding it stretches the length of the city. Our girls had peered into caves, climbed over ruins and statues, and turned somersaults in the grass, but late in the day, their feet began to drag. Still, we marched down the street under a sweltering sun.

"I don't think there's a ginkgo tree anywhere in Weimar," Mira said.

"We need to get going," Dave added. "We've got hundreds of kilo-meters ahead of us."

"Right." I kept walking. "And we need lunch and something to drink. Just help me find the cemetery."

"I'm so tired!" Olivia whined.

"I'll buy you Fanta and ice cream," I promised. I desperately wanted to see Goethe and Schiller's twin coffins, which were laid side by side in a vault populated with royal bodies. The guidebook informed us that Goethe convinced the Duke to erect the noble chapel, with a space re-served for the authors to rest in mutual peace. They say Schiller revived Goethe's passion for writing. He looked past the fame and saw Goethe's promise.

In "Wanderer's Nightsong (Another One)," Goethe writes, "Above all the summits is silence. In all the treetops you sense hardly a breath. The birds are quiet in the woods. Just wait, soon you shall keep silence too." As a youth, Goethe wrote these words on the wall of a mountain-side cabin. Fifty years later, after his last birthday, Goethe rode with his grandsons to show them his writing on the wall. I picture the elderly Goethe recalling the dear friend he's missed for long ages. He wasn't looking for joy anymore, only peace. I understood his loneliness. That's why we were still walking.

When we finally stepped inside the cool, dim mausoleum, I hesitat-ed. *Do I want to spend seven euros for this?* I wondered.

Aloud, I said, "Do you think that's all it is? Just the two coffins downstairs?" Dave gave a lackluster shrug in response.

The lady behind the glass booth stared at me. My family stood at wits' end a few feet away as I pushed my coins across the counter. We walked to a small sign inside the velvet rope, and I read the tale in German: Under cover of night, Schiller's body was dug up from its original common grave. Scientists confirmed the identity of his skull, and Goethe, long years after his beloved friend's passing, held the skull in his hand, declaring it to be so.

During the Second World War, officials from nearby Buchenwald (formerly the "birch forest" where Goethe wrote poems) sent both coffins to Nuremberg for destruction; only a Nazi doctor who hid the boxes saved them. What Nazis couldn't accomplish, modern science did—DNA testing proved the bones belonged not to Schiller but four entirely unrelated people.

As I read this, my thoughts reeled. Downstairs in the small crypt, I would see the receptacle of Germany's great lifeless hero, Goethe. But the second box, the one bearing Schiller's name, was empty. We'd spent the equivalent of ten bucks for the privilege of learning what I would've remembered if I'd paid attention: Schiller never appears where he's expected. His magical presence is defined by his absence. Likewise, I'd never encounter joy in the present by tracking its past locations.

If I wanted to love actively, I'd have to look in new places.

# 18

## Birdwatching in Karlsruhe / Vogelbeobachtung

"In one thousand meters, turn left on Gan-del-sheem-er-strass," proclaimed the voice of our rental GPS in its feminine British accent. *Strass* rhymed with *ass*. The American voice mangled street names even more, so we went with British, since Dave doesn't know German.

In real German, the word *Gondelsheimerstraße* flows like music and the *e* isn't silent. You just have to sound out the syllables—*Gone-dels-high-mare-straw-saw*.

I spoke the name aloud to no one in particular. The girls chattered on in a backseat game. Dave kept his eyes fixed on the road. *Gone-dels-high-mare-straw-saw*—a left turn up the hill. It should've been simple. But it wasn't.

"There's a *Vogelpark* you can walk to from here," Julia had suggested that morning—a bird park, one of many throughout the country. To be honest, I'm not sure why Germans have all these bird parks. Maybe something to do with their love of nature?

The closest *Vogelpark* Dave and I found on the Internet was a few kilometers away. So after lunch, we set out by car. When we didn't find it where the GPS promised, we backtracked to Gondelsheimerstrasse and turned left again, a snap decision that led us higher and higher on a two-lane highway out of town—with no sign of a *Vogelpark*.

"Recalculating." Again and again the unflappable voice told us to turn around. After the fifth time, I shut the contraption off.

There was no shoulder to pull over onto and enough cars coming from the other direction to keep Dave from making a three-point-turn, especially with another car barreling down on us from behind. When Dave slowed to let that car pass, its horn blared.

Dave began shouting: at the car, the road, the GPS. "I can't turn around. Back off. Agh!" His face had turned bright red.

The girls stopped playing in the backseat. At seven, they knew enough to stay quiet.

"*Scheisse!*" their father bellowed.

At last we came to a small dirt road. Dave decelerated just enough to make the quick turn. He slammed the car to a stop, threw it into park, and took several deep breaths. Nobody said a word.

When several minutes had passed and he saw no cars in either direction, Dave put the car into gear. He edged the compact Fiat back and forth across the road. Once it faced the other way, we continued in silence, all the way down Gondelsheimerstrasse, back onto the main road that brought us to Julia and Hugh's house. Once there, Dave pulled onto the steep sidewalk, cranked on the emergency brake, and went inside to lie down.

·❧·

We had seventeen days left in Germany. And I needed to make the trip worthwhile.

At scheduled group events, Dave wrangled our daughters. Mostly they seemed to have fun. But what did they do on an average day? Three mornings a week, I drove to school for homeroom with my students. Dave stayed behind with Mira and Olivia, trying to keep them entertained and make sure they didn't cause too much damage in the backyard.

At least the girls knew enough now to stay out of the fishpond. Two years before, on the day we arrived, Julia and Hugh had given them the run of the place. In response, the girls demolished the lily pads and terrorized the goldfish. Julia's heirloom peach tree, minus its lowest limb, nonetheless survived. On our second day, she'd wisely bought a giant inflatable pool.

Another day, Mira and Olivia had left their mesh shoes outside during a downpour. I'd found them the next morning, one blue pair and one gold, strewn across the lawn. Picking up a shoe, I grimaced. The girls couldn't wear these sopping shoes into town. And how had it gotten so filthy?

Then I realized: that's not dirt! I squealed and hurled the shoe at the ground.

Slugs covered the soles and burrowed into all four toes. Julia came out of the house when she heard my commotion. She grabbed each shoe in turn, wiped the slugs off with deft movements, then removed the insoles to make sure they were gone. Only then would I pick up the shoes so I could run them under the hose and wash away slug poo. The backyard was a nice place to visit, but there was nowhere else for the girls to play. Small wonder they got into trouble.

This time, Hugh had laid down the law when he found the girls walking on the field of pebbles that covered his garage roof. "That is very dangerous," I heard him bellow. "Don't you ever do that again."

I needed to get us out of that house, living the German experience. Apparently, that meant *Vogelparks*.

*♡*

Once I'd given Dave enough time alone in our family's shared room, I went in and turned on Hugh's old computer, hoping to salvage the ill-conceived idea.

"I found a listing for another *Vogelpark* past the train station. Shall we give it another try?"

He peered out from under his forearm. "Sure."

On our second attempt, we parked near athletic fields on a dead-end road. A wooden sign said *Vogelpark*, and we took off in the most obvious direction, a wide path past tall pines. Eventually we crossed a pedestrian bridge over the Autobahn. Cars zoomed beneath us.

"This can't be right," I said. "We've gone too far."

"Yep." Dave sighed. "Let's go back."

Julia laughed when she heard about our misadventures. "I struggled with that same hill when I was learning to drive, only I had to use a stick shift." She shook her head. "The bird park I meant is much closer to home." We agreed to try again the following day.

I could've written our misadventure off as a bad day. But we all knew the truth. I went to look for Dave and found him sitting in the leather easy chair in our basement room.

"Do you want to be done with Karlsruhe?" I swallowed hard against the lump in my throat.

He looked up. "I don't want to come back."

I inhaled deep. "I've got to do at least one more round. I've promised people back home. I've recruited them."

He nodded but didn't reply.

"These exchanges keep kids signing up for German. I can't stop now."

"No," he said, quiet. "It makes sense for you to go."

I stared out through the sliding glass door. "But I've asked enough of you," I half asked, half said.

Dave nodded again.

"And our kids need childhood summers." I cradled my cheeks in my hands. "Other than ongoing travel for their mother's job."

"Right."

The conversation went so fast, the matter decided. I'd return in two years without them. I'd find someone to chaperone with me. So why did I feel caged in?

*⟨⟩*

I never drove in Germany until I started leading homerooms. There are so many foreign rules of engagement. Often within villages, buildings facing each other stand so close the road narrows down to two lanes, one for driving, one for parking. Cars from the parked-car side must yield. They find an open space and pull over for oncoming traffic, sometimes onto the sidewalk. All visible cars from the other direction must pass by first before they continue.

This feels like a game of chicken, weaving in and out of traffic. So in Julia's village, I carefully scanned the road. But as I hit the stretch that brought me to school the next valley over, the feeling of freedom came over me. My body swayed in a dance with the winding curves. I was going places all by myself.

⌒

At school I waited in a classroom over the *Mensa*, a word that in America means an organization for smart people but in Germany is a cafeteria. I was making a mental note of false cognates—seemingly similar words with different intentions. They would be the first things my students noticed.

I watched them arrive in the plaza below. They stayed close to their host partners until the other Amis appeared. Soon their voices overlapped in the hallway. They burst into the classroom, where I stood ready at the kelly green chalkboard.

"I can't open the doors," one girl said.

"Right?" said a boy across the room. "I feel so incredibly stupid."

"And so tired!" said another girl. "Yesterday I fell asleep on the train." Students giggled and nodded in agreement.

One boy added, "My little brother speaks German lightning fast, then shouts out my name. He's four, but it feels like I'm the child."

The room erupted with laughter. This is what I was there for—I could relate because *I'd been there*. I reminded them of the following day's scavenger hunt, downtown near the pyramid. Their host partners would know where to go. The bell rang, and they streamed out the door.

⌒

A few moments later, I was savoring my *Laugenstange* (a pretzel roll slathered in butter) when I heard a voice.

"Frau Hallberg?"

I looked up. A sweet girl stood in the doorframe, dark brown bangs skirting her eyes. She and I often exchanged pleasantries. Now she hesitated. "I'm worried about Lisa. Her partner Lisa refuses to speak English. They haven't gone to activities all weekend."

I winced. I'd paired the Lisas myself, based purely on the coincidence of their names. (Why I thought this was a good idea, I'm not sure. There were seven Lisas in our second-grade class, my old friend Lisa sometimes reminds me, her perky voice still tinged with frustration.)

"So it hasn't gotten better," I said. "Has she spoken to her host mom?"

The girl shook her head. "And I don't know what to do." Her voice wobbled. "She's my friend, but I want to have fun. This is my first trip to Germany too."

"You've been a good friend." I felt a fluttering in my chest. "Take care of yourself. I'll talk with them after the scavenger hunt."

I replayed this conversation on the drive home. When I was recruiting and pairing partners, I relied on alchemy. I'd gush about Eva, and how we'd been friends all these years. As if I could guarantee lifelong friendships. And yet, I'd never stand again in their place, befriending Germany—or each other—for the first time. This wasn't my past. It was their present. And still I felt responsible for making their experience smoother than mine.

Back at the house, Dave had the girls ready. This time he knew where we were going. Hugh had pointed out the right *Vogelpark* on a walk to a pub for a couple of pints. We ambled down a side road, beside a rushing stream. At last we arrived at wooden stairs, cut into the hillside. They led to a terraced collection of pens.

A display at the entrance listed several rules. I translated aloud while Dave called out his alternate version: "Do not taunt the birds. Do not mock the birds. Do not poison the birds."

There was a pair of neon-green lovebirds with coral heads. A buttery cockatoo. A black raven with a golden beak and feet and shocks of gold and white feathers. Inside the cages, some birds puffed themselves up. Some ignored us. Some stared us straight in the eyes. We left through another entrance between two tall beams with a plank between them. When we turned back, we could read the words carved there: "*Vogelfreunde 1958.*"

Bird friends since 1958. A decade after the end of devastating war, people had restored their lives enough to build this bird sanctuary. Maybe it was a testament to their humanity: The soul of Germany wasn't destroyed. Hope remained.

There were three tombstones past that, over a century old. On the road into town, we looked out over the whole village at hilly meadows closed in behind buildings and fences, all crammed together. Across the valley, houses gave way to spacious hillside again. We continued into the center of town and bought ice cream.

*I'll miss this when they're not here,* I realized.

⌀

The dribbling rain that greeted us as we exited the train had increased to a downpour by the time forty of us converged on the Marktplatz, huddled under canopies near the pyramid.

Julia and Sabine arrived together. "If this rain doesn't let up," Julia said, "the scavenger hunt won't work."

"I think the kids would prefer to go shopping." Even wet, Sabine's hair looked sleek.

"Okay," I said. "Would one of you be willing to stay and talk with the Lisas? My Lisa's friend says it's not going well."

Julia and Sabine exchanged glances. When they were in the States,

I'd argued for them to replace my Lisa's host partner due to lack of chemistry. A heavy weight sat in the pit of my stomach.

"I'll be happy to help," Sabine said, voice smooth as ever.

After several more minutes in the damp chill, we said goodbye, and the students scattered to make the most of their evening. Except my family—we went into a nearby bakery where Dave sat at a table with Mira and Olivia.

We teachers and students chose another table. The German Lisa sat beside Sabine, with her wide-open eyes, perfectly arched eyebrows, and close-cropped burgundy hair. On the other side, the American Lisa and I faced them. With my shaggy brown mom hair, frizzy from the rain, I felt dowdy and out of my depth.

Sabine and I carefully chose our English words while the two teenagers looked at their hands, at us, and occasionally at each other as we navigated their issues for forty-five minutes.

"We haven't met up with the others since I got here," said the American Lisa.

"You never answer us when we ask you questions," said the German Lisa.

"I don't understand you. You ask me in German, and mine's not that good." Both girls wore pained expressions.

"There's clearly some miscommunication," said Sabine. "A difference of perspectives."

I leaned in. "It's much harder with two languages and two cultures. What if you both ask more questions? Ask for what you need, ask what the other needs. And share your reasons why—in English when German won't work."

"I think I can ask more questions," said American Lisa.

"I will try to explain better," said German Lisa.

"That sounds like an excellent plan," said Sabine.

The Lisas got up and walked into the rain, looking more like strangers than ever. I went to rescue my family at the other table, where Olivia and Mira sat squirming, bickering, and whining.

"Have they eaten anything?" I asked.

"No." Dave glared. "I didn't buy them food because we had plans for dinner."

He was right; we'd wanted to look for a nearby restaurant where they'd serve us *Schnitzel* and fries and a little bag of Haribo gummies. Instead, we invited Sabine to join us at the mall, where we settled for slices of pizza you could get anywhere in America.

Sabine tried to engage us in conversation, commenting on our day, on the lovely pizza. But it was no use. My family had wilted. Dave stared into space, and the girls picked at their food. I managed to be pleasant until we said goodbye. Then the four of us started for home, dodging torrents of rain until our streetcar arrived.

❧

An hour later, I was standing with my daughters on the latest in a series of platforms, waiting for one of the trains that would take us back to Julia's. A pigeon walked toward the far end of the platform where Dave stood motionless, staring at a large diagram of train lines.

The German word for pigeon—*Taube*—is the same as the word for dove. German has a way of getting to essential truths. A bearer of peace is sometimes just an annoying pest. It depends on your perspective. Maybe that was me with my exchanges. I only knew my husband was standing far away while I watched over our cranky girls.

The rain slowed to a dribble again. As the express train approached, I felt its momentum, about to pass us at full speed. The wind took hold of my hair. I grabbed on to my children, pressing them close to my sides as I took a step back.

The rumble of the train startled one of the pigeons nestled by the edge of the platform. It suddenly fluttered into the rush of the train. I covered my face with my hands and shut my eyes. When I dared to look around, I saw the pigeon's lifeless body behind us, by the adjacent track. There was no blood, only feathers.

It took several long moments for the girls to register shock, then sorrow. They started to wail.

"The birds!" Olivia finally exclaimed, wise beyond her nearly eight years. "Why is it always the birds?"

I was helpless, my hands still grasping my face. Dave rushed over to see what had happened, to rub the girls' backs and coo soothing words. Another train slowed to a halt before us.

We got on board.

# 19

## Return to the Source / Donauquelle

I'd compromised in so many ways as a mother. I taught German even when my children were babies. At age three, they began riding with me to the town across the river, where I dropped them off on my way to school. To lighten the mood, we often set conversations to melodies made up on the way. We could keep our favorite German song going for miles:

Marmor, Stein, und Eisen bricht. Aber unsere Liebe nicht.
Alles, alles geht vorbei.
Doch wir sind uns treu. Everybody now!
Marble, stone, and iron breaks. But not our love.
Everything, everything passes away.
To each other we are true. Every-body-now!

The song reminded me of an old photograph of Eva and me, taken in Athens on our trip through Greece. We stand on a hillside that faces the Acropolis, arms around each other's shoulders. And a tiny keepsake still graces my dresser, two yellow plaster birds nestled together. Eva left it on my bedside table soon after we returned to Donaueschingen. On a heart-shaped piece of paper, she had written, "Greece says hi."

Certainly my friendship with Eva is a testament to faithful endurance.

That's the effect I was going for as a mom.

By 2011, my second-graders and I had our routine down. Curbside every morning at seven thirty, each daughter leaned forward from the backseat so we could exchange a hug and kiss, then look together into the rearview mirror. While they piled out the door, I gave last-minute instructions they simultaneously assented to and brushed off. I would watch them walk through the school door and down the sunlit hall, heads bobbing side by side.

After they disappeared around the corner, I'd set off, relieved to have gotten us so far.

I often called Mom when I reached my next destination, three minutes away. She would reassure me that yes, my daughters would grow into responsible and kind young women who remember to put on socks and brush their teeth without arguments. It helped me relax into my own routine until I picked the girls up nine hours later.

One evening in the spring, as we prepared for this second Germany trip, a boy called after me in the parking lot, "You're going to get a surprise."

"I hope I like it," I called back.

When I reached the basement, Mira's normally chilly and reserved teacher cornered me. She was livid. Both girls had forgotten their lunches for the field trip—again.

Before I could apologize, she launched into a litany about Olivia, who'd lost her temper. Two boys had knocked over the castle she was constructing from blocks. Mira's teacher ignored the boys to subdue Olivia, who railed against repression of creativity. Then Olivia's teacher jumped in. Chaos ensued.

I would've sided with my daughter, if only she hadn't gotten so out of hand. And reminded me of myself.

I felt my eyes narrow and my face harden as my daughter approached.

In the car, where all serious negotiations take place, I began to explain the rules for the umpteenth time, and I lost it. My accusations rained down: "You do not ever yell at a teacher. Does it help losing your temper? How does it help?"

I could hear how ridiculous I sounded. Crossing back over the river, I finally landed on, "I'm sorry. I don't know what to do. And I'm afraid I'm a terrible mother."

From the backseat, Mira stopped me short. "Just because you don't know what to do doesn't mean you're a terrible mother."

Her calmness threw me. "What?"

"Just because you don't know what to do," Olivia repeated, "doesn't make you a terrible mother. You're a good mother."

"What do I do, then?" My voice was very small.

"First, you give us guidance," said Mira. "Which you already do. And you hold us and tell us you love us. After that, it's on us."

In my daughters, I see myself, but far less cautious. During this second exchange trip, they discovered snails perched on stones and tree bark. They lined them up on Julia's wooden picnic table, round spiraling shells striped in brown, yellow, white, and black.

"I don't mind," Julia said, "as long as you throw them over the fence."

Mira and Olivia made up their own rules for the snails. As a test of courage, they would hold each one by its shell and jump with it off a short wall. The winner—and most courageous snail—never retreated into its shell. Those that did were disqualified.

I could've used some of that courage going into our final weekend.

Since I knew the girls wouldn't join me on future exchanges, our visit to Mami and Papi's house in Donaueschingen loomed especially large. It was our last, best chance to solidify a lasting friendship with Eva's daughters.

Everything hinged on Sophia and Carlotta's emerging English. If everything went as planned, maybe one day I'd show them around the Twin Cities. Someday—I hoped—when Mira and Olivia knew enough German, I'd entrust them to Eva in Hamburg. But I knew full well shared language wasn't enough. The girls knew how much Eva meant to me. I was counting on that to keep them in line for their sleepover with Sophia, also nearly eight.

And what about Eva's oldest daughter, Carlotta? At eleven, she'd likely stay in another room. Even on our first visit, she'd often sat with the adults, slumped into a chair and reading a book.

Olivia must've shared my nervousness; in the backseat on our drive down, she threw up into a plastic bag I handed her just in time. She'd promised to write Sophia after our first stay, and then two years had passed. But as we entered through the kitchen door, all the girls ran off into the house, friends reunited once more.

Mami greeted Dave and me in her Prussian way, at once attentive and formal, then ushered us to the dining room for a full meal, placed on the table in a hurry, the same as ever.

After the meal, Eva suggested we spend our day at an amusement park, named for the Schwarzwald.

"It's traditional for this region," she said. I recalled our days at American theme parks, populated by cheerful fantasy creatures, programmed and plastered with shiny logos. This was a different kind of park, distinctly more German, with sturdy buildings framed in wood, and with real goats, sheep, and deer—animals native to the Schwarzwald.

Deciding which way to go, Eva and I must've looked like moms on a first play date, each dressed in jeans and a button-down blouse, each wearing a sweater, carrying a bag, and leaning against the railing. Meanwhile, all five kids piled into a yellow go-kart and raced around the track.

When we were younger, Eva had called Americans superficial, with our need to make everything so pleasant, to talk when words weren't called for. But those words grounded me. I felt awkward without them as the kids chased back and forth.

"So you made it to Weimar," Eva said, breaking the silence. "Did you like it?" We were waiting by the log ride. A few feet away, preteen Carlotta leaned against the railing, staring into space.

I glanced at Eva. "Did you know that Schiller died at forty-five?"

Just then the three younger girls ran up, still dripping, all begging in their native tongues for one more turn on the ride. So much for deep conversation.

Once we reached the playground, Carlotta came alive, bounding onto merry-go-rounds and teeter-totters like ones from my childhood, long since disappeared from the American experience. The four girls climbed into a giant hollow barrel, mounted on its side and open at both ends. They ran for a minute as the barrel tossed them about, emerging dizzy and joyful.

I could only see the danger. I pictured one of them falling, being hit, being hurt, but I forced myself to stand clear. I envied them, fearless and free.

"You would never find those contraptions on an American playground," I announced as my kids climbed into our backseat for the ride home to Mami and Papi's.

"Why not?" Mira asked.

"Well, it's like the *Kindereier*. They're just chocolate eggs with little plastic capsules containing toys, but they're illegal in America."

"What's wrong with *Kindereier*?" Olivia asked.

"They're choking hazards," I began, then stopped myself. I'd adored *Kindereier* from the first time Eva introduced me to them.

♫

After dinner, Eva escorted Dave and me to the door. "You get breakfast at the hotel, so why don't you eat first and come by afterward." She looked exhausted.

The day had played itself out, but night hadn't yet fallen. So Dave and I checked in at our hotel, then crossed a wooden footbridge over a babbling brook, and wandered into the sleepy streets of town.

I recognized the buildings more by impression than memory. At a crossroads, I looked for the road where Eva's friend Claudi had lived.

"I think the post office is down that way," I told Dave. "You know, that's where I first realized I'd never speak perfect German."

"That's what's so great about Latin." Dave chuckled. "Unless you're a priest, no one expects you to speak it."

"And the train station where I ran off to Karlsruhe. That's got to be there too."

Donaueschingen stood just out of my grasp. Like a place I once passed through rather than one that changed my life. Nobody would even remember, nothing would show I was ever here. Near a pale green café I once frequented, a group of other youths stood at a skatepark beneath the overpass.

I didn't belong in Donaueschingen anymore.

Eva didn't either. She'd started her family in Hamburg, at the other end of Germany, where she and Anton ran a thriving medical practice. But she taught her daughters to read in the English she adored.

To tell the truth, Eva had never had much to say about the Schwarzwald. In letters over the years, she'd written about Berlin and great German cities to the east. Exotic travel to foreign lands. Almost immediately after I arrived at the house on Geschwister-Scholl-Straße, Eva had spirited me away on that three-week school trip through Greece.

This place was always too small for Eva. When I was seventeen, it empowered me.

At the hotel entrance, I took one last look back toward town. Sometimes a small start is good enough. The Donauquelle, source of the legendary Danube, inhabits a grotto you could easily overlook, beneath the shadow of a mustard-yellow baroque church. It's a round pool framed in ornate concrete and metal, its bright blue water punctuated by moss and discarded coins, snails perched on the side. As a teen, Eva laughed about its lofty aspirations. I saw that little basin and imagined its potential.

*⌀*

When I woke in the hotel the following morning, a thought occurred to me.

Just before we'd left for Germany, I'd heard a *Rolling Stone* interviewer talking on the radio. He'd said he returned a second day for all his interviews. The first time, you see the person at surface level. By the time you return the second day, people let their guard down, and then you see the real person.

It occurred to me that it had always been true with Eva too, and surely her children as well. It took us a day to get used to each other again. But we only had these two days. Was it enough for the connection between our daughters to take root?

I adored Eva. Our friendship had survived over time and in many places. That didn't mean our girls would continue that tradition.

I shared my theories with Dave over breakfast.

"Maybe Eva and I will always need two days to warm up," I said.

He took a sip of coffee and nodded.

"Do you think she'll want to foster their friendship?" I asked. "Because the girls will only maintain this connection if we help them make it happen."

"I don't know," he said, taking another sip of his coffee. "I guess today we'll find out."

That morning did feel different. From her parents' house, we followed Eva's car into town and parked beneath some trees near the castle park. She and I recalled old times and watched ducks swim in the stream while the younger girls scrambled up a tree. Afterward, we ordered pizza at a Turkish restaurant, where all the girls sat together at one table.

Sitting with me at the next table over, Dave and Eva began trading tales about their Greek studies.

"Do you remember when I lost my retainer?" I asked her. "Right before we got to Athens? Everyone was waiting on the bus, and you told me I should forget it?"

"I was so mad at you." Eva laughed. "That whole time, my beloved classics teacher was digging through garbage cans out back."

A calm came over me. "I felt so clueless on that trip, like I was weighing you down."

"That must have been painful." Eva met my eyes across the table.

"Are you kidding?" I held her gaze. "I wouldn't have missed it for the world. That trip changed my life."

"We should get together again," Dave said as I went up to pay the bill. And with that, he and Eva began comparing destinations.

❧

Back at the house, I settled into a chair to talk with Papi, to discuss politics and history and places we'd been. He'd just finished showing me photos from his trip with Mami to see the Dresdner *Frauenkirche*—Cathedral of Our Lady. It had been demolished in firebombs during the final days of World War II, then restored half a century later from fragments pulled from the ashes. I was about to start rounding up the girls for our long trip back to Karlsruhe when I heard Mami's sudden cry from the front door: *"Ach du Liebe! Was machst du deiner Oma? Was tust du mir?"*—Oh, you dear thing! What are you doing to your grandma? What are you doing to me?

I ran to ask what was wrong.

*"Ich liebe meine Enkelkinder. Aber schau mal, Amy, schau was sie da getan haben!"*—I love my grandchildren. But just look what they've done!

There in the corner, on the sheltered step outside, I saw a pile of grass and bright green leaves that formed a little mound, almost like a nest.

"*Was is'n das?*" I asked—What is that?

"*Schnecken!*" she said mournfully, shaking her head. "*Die haben da Schnecken gesammelt!*" Mira, Sophia, and Olivia had gathered snails from all over the yard into a little snail haven on the front step, to protect them from the rain. Then the girls ran off into the house, leaving the door wide open.

In the meantime, the snails had left the nest and crept inside the front entry, with a few stragglers still crossing the threshold. "*Die müssen ja weg!*" Mami said—They have got to go.

Each of the three girls, when we finally got them downstairs to answer for themselves, smiled the way you do when you're caught but only a little sorry. Carlotta, the oldest, watched from the corner, shaking her head and smirking.

Snails. Of course. As if to remind me that however slowly we move across time, we will all get where we're going eventually.

I was certain Sophia would get to Minnesota.

*♆*

A little later, my family stood in the street outside the house, where we hugged each member of Eva's assembled family before climbing into the car. As we pulled away, I saw them lined up in the rearview mirror, waving: Eva, her parents, and her two younger children. All except eleven-year-old Carlotta. She was running after us at top speed.

The girls and I turned to watch her out the rear window as she ran down the street, growing ever smaller until we rounded the corner and she disappeared from view.

# 2O

## So Long, Farewell / Auf Wiedersehen . . .

The evening after we got back from Donaueschingen, my family had dinner with Julia and Sabine at a centuries-old restaurant in Durlach. Karl lived in this inner-ring suburb before riding into the fields and dreaming his fateful dream—and, as all the locals know, leaving his wife behind. In our own little candlelit room with thick white walls and heavy wooden beams, we ate *Maultaschen*—dumplings called "feed-bags"—and *Rotkohl*—red cabbage—specialties from the Baden region. Walking back to the parking lot with Sabine on a narrow sidewalk in the dark, I told her I felt tired. Dave and the girls walked ahead of us with Julia.

"Dave's tired too," I said. "He's not coming back next time."

"Oh," Sabine said, her mouth rounding as the sound escaped. "I didn't realize that."

From my perspective, our struggles were on display for everyone to see. I felt certain my students saw my pinched expression and iso-lation—on all sides. My worry was mounting. And unlike last time, very few students found my kids or me particularly cute. On our recent visit to the Triberg waterfalls on the side of a Black Forest mountain, supposedly Germany's highest falls, Mira and Olivia had bickered on the bus until Dave and I separated them. We'd arrived at the site just as I realized the persistent odor I smelled came from Olivia's only pair of tennis shoes.

While Julia and Sabine marched ahead across a wooden suspension bridge, I'd lingered behind, asking a student to take a few pictures of my family.

When I turned to see the waterfall, I gasped. The bus driver had climbed onto the rock face, where water poured down behind him. Several of the German teens and most of my students had followed, edging their way out there, including a girl on crutches. My liability insurance suddenly felt very flimsy.

"Get back in here! *Now!*" I screamed at the top of my lungs, barely audible above the raging waters. The delighted students smiled and waved.

"Take our picture first," one called back, gesturing as if holding a camera. Others cheered and imitated him. Only I was trembling.

I looked at Dave, who shrugged, a scowl etched on his face. So we took a couple pictures of the kids on the boulders, white streams cascading behind them. "Now get back here," I screamed again. "Carefully!"

One by one they stepped across the wet stones, my heart pounding until every last one set foot on the walkway and headed back to the bus. I glared at the driver, chagrinned at myself too.

At our rustic lodge that evening, the entire group wandered onto a hilltop after dinner, where the American and German kids leapfrogged and chased each other, the sky spreading out before us, rosy and orange, and joy overtook me.

Sabine snapped a picture of Dave and me standing on that

mountaintop, backlit by the plummy sky in the last moments before sunset. She planned to publish it in the local newspaper, along with a glowing article about the exchange between our schools—expanded to include two Minnesota high schools. Even when she took the photo, I recognized a different unmistakable promise in that image.

After she walked away, I swept my arms wide open, spinning as I sang in my finest falsetto warble, "The hills are alive with the sound of music!"

A few of my students laughed aloud. Dave smiled his recognition. Mira and Olivia took their own little spins. But not a single German understood the reference. It was a message to myself, anyway.

I remembered laughing with my fellow teens at the edge of a lock in Germany's industrial region, and how I photographed the rounded trajectory of one boy peeing into the waters. We were young and carefree and found ourselves hilarious. Even as recently as the previous exchange, Dave and I had chuckled while talking my students off the ledge of a castle in Baden Baden, where we found them each posing in turn. That was their nature. It couldn't be helped.

⌘

Following dinner in Durlach, I couldn't sleep. I was thinking about a Moninger beer coaster I'd grabbed at the restaurant: "*Die Probleme im Leben entstehen daraus, daß man etwas sät und etwas ganz anderes ernten möchte.*"—The troubles in life arise when one sows one thing and wants to reap something quite different.

A few hours later, after restless dreams, I awakened before dawn. I got up and moved to kiss Olivia, sprawled across the shared full mattress. Then I maneuvered to the other side, careful not to disturb her sleep. As I hugged Mira, she rolled over, throwing her arm across me. She murmured, "Mom. Mommy."

I settled onto the bed, cuddling up to her, listening to her sweet breath flow in measured cadences. I remembered the silent promise I made when she took her first breath: *There you are. I've been looking for you. Now that you're here, everything will be all right.*

More than ever, I needed to believe it.

*⌀*

During this visit, I'd met up again with an old friend named Dani. She had attended my hometown high school the same year Eva was there. Over the summer of 1987, after I returned to America and before she returned to West Germany, Dani and I had hung out for a few weeks. We visited German summer school as guest speakers—my first teaching experience. Since then, Dani had married a Brit and established an impressive career with international nongovernmental organizations.

I asked her if, after so many years of using English professionally and at home, she ever felt as comfortable speaking it as she did her native German.

"You know," Dani said, "I never do." Her husband could maintain a conversation while listening to the BBC on television, tracking back and forth, but she couldn't. "I just can't focus on two things in English. I don't think I ever will."

*⌀*

I thought about it constantly, how I felt my attention torn in that way.

That final week, Dave, our daughters, and my students rode to an adventure park in a Karlsruhe suburb. We strapped on helmets and harnesses and spent the day navigating ropes courses strung between treetops.

Dave clipped his carabineers onto cables and stepped off ledges without a moment of hesitation, our daughters flitting between us, calling to students as we passed.

We were finally sharing an experience, all twenty of us.

Ten minutes before the meeting time, Olivia and I made the ill-advised decision to make one last run through a new course. We'd hardly set off when I realized it would take us a good twenty minutes or more. My blood raced, but with no way to turn back, we plowed forward, traversing the canopy and transferring our tethers at each tree, even riding a surfboard suspended midair, graceful and urgent until our last zip line.

Dave stood at the base, surrounded by my students. His eyebrows were pinched, and he held his arms tight across his chest. When we reached them, he spoke in a low growl. "The whole group was waiting for you. We're hot, tired, and hungry. I promised Mira ice cream, but you have the money."

I didn't reply, doing my best to mask my roiling emotions. I returned my harness to the counter, then went to buy two ice creams. After checking that nobody was missing, we started down the winding road to the station, with Dave far ahead of everyone.

On the train, he rode by himself. Mira sat, sticky and grimy, on the lap of a redheaded boy with an uncomfortable expression, while Olivia climbed across the girl beside him.

"Mira, Olivia!" I finally said. "Come sit here by me."

Once my family reached our stop, students safely out of earshot, I turned to face Dave. "I know I made a mistake, but that was humiliating, you ignoring me like that."

He directed his full attention toward me. "I've done everything you've asked me to. And you want everyone speaking German, so mostly I'm keeping to myself. I don't even like ropes courses, but I made an effort to enjoy myself, and I did it for you."

It felt as if the ground had dropped out below my feet. "I'm sorry," I managed. "I had no business taking that last course. And thank you."

"It's fine." He nodded and marched toward the car. The girls fell silently in behind him, while I stayed several paces back. On the rest of the icy car ride home, my cheeks burned. I thought about how much I'd accomplished during the exchange. I'd held meetings and composed emails and handled the money and the paperwork.

But while I might have looked confident leading the charge, I relied on Dave and our daughters to reflect the meaning from these German adventures, the same way I once counted on Eva. I could do the exchange without them, but where would I find the courage and strength to carry on my charade? Why would I want to?

♂

Anytime I caught one of my students using their German, I pulled out what I called *Stempelzettel*—colorful squares of paper imprinted with "*Fabelhaft*" and "*Ausgezeichnet*"—Fabulous! Outstanding! I created piles every morning before leaving the house, and I spent the entire trip passing them out. "Aha!" I would say. "Deutsch! Here's your reward." I reminded each student to save them for the prize drawing I would hold at the end of the trip.

For my students, I bought four gift certificates to Media Markt. For the Germans, I chose blue erasers bearing American flags and the words New York, the state all Germans dreamed of visiting; white-out editing pens, for the many corrections to our German; tins of *Denkdrops mit Vitamin C für Besserdenker*—lemon and orange "thinking" drops for better thinkers; a package of *Kung Fu Panda 2* glue sticks; and a box of my favorite Yogurette chocolates with strawberry yogurt filling and English yogurt spelling. I left the store standing a little taller, carrying this bag of items I could explain with funny anecdotes.

As the German partners arrived at our farewell party, I asked them to write their names on their *Stempelzettel* and put them into a box. But almost everyone looked at me with blank expressions. I recognized their empty stares from when Julia asked the group who would volunteer to set up this party while she worked late at conferences.

When only a handful of students pulled slips from their wallets, I stifled my urge to scream. I pictured all those carefully chosen prizes.

In the end, I smiled extra big and tore a page from my notebook. "How many *Stempelzettel* did you earn?" I asked each of the German teens, handing them fresh scraps to write their names on. I would not cart my prizes back to America, nor would I hunt down the cups and napkins nobody thought to bring.

Throughout the evening, parents came to sit with me and talk about their families, ask about mine, or tell me some cute or funny or touching thing their American guest had done. I was at my most charming when I explained each of the prizes to the group, and everyone laughed at just the right moment.

After handing out the prizes, I asked my students to join me at the front of the room and share their favorite moments. The depth of their words—the details they'd noticed—touched my heart, all variations on a theme: You made me delicious food. You helped me learn German. You brought me chocolate. You laughed with me, not at me. You made me feel loved. You're family now. The Germans responded with applause and oohs and nods of agreement.

At last Julia rose to say how I'd carried the exchange all on my own in America, how in fact I carried an entire German program in two separate high schools. "This thing has changed so many lives," she said, and I knew in my heart it was true.

I stood and gave a speech, completely impromptu. In grammatically perfect German, I found the words to express my gratitude for all these people had done for us. For me.

Looking out, I saw Dave, Mira, and Olivia, their eyes trained on me, swelling with pride. I also saw all those students, who counted on me because I convinced them to trust me.

Mere days before, I'd stood in front of a class of German sixth graders, several with siblings who'd already seen Minnesota. I told those children I'd love to welcome them to America in four years. But deep down, I was dying to tell someone—anyone—the truth.

I wasn't coming back to Karlsruhe.

# 21

## Shadow Side / Schattenseite

No sooner did we arrive at the baggage claim of the Minneapolis-St. Paul Airport, greeted by cheers from the delighted assembly of parents, than our entire group scattered, waving as they left my family standing beside our luggage.

On their way out the door, they called out, "*Danke, Frau Hallberg. Auf Wiedersehen, Frau Hallberg.*" Then the echoes of their cries died down, and we stood alone. In the deafening silence, reality sank in. I would soon reenter a life that felt less and less like my own, my once-beloved job now soul-crushingly hard.

Returning to our suburban home, I observed my estrangement from the carefully chosen colors on our walls: the mossy green I painted in the upper hallway a week before leaving, the longstanding indigo-blue in the back hallway. I noticed the oddness of the beige carpet underfoot and my own clean laundry, still folded in baskets on the living room floor. The emptiness stirring within me felt so much deeper than jet lag, rising from the core of my being.

A few hours later, Wolfgang's canine breathing startled me awake. The clock glowed 3:21, ungodly early. Despite this, I got up. I wandered into my writing studio, turned on the light, and closed the door. I laid down on the daybed. My mind stirred in the rushing silence of night touching morning.

From atop a white display cabinet, Schiller gazed down at me. He was the only souvenir I'd bothered to unpack. Studying his plaster visage, I worried what people would say about me at not one, but two high schools when they heard I was abandoning the exchange.

Under Schiller's watchful eyes, I rested on the daybed all week, an ice pack keeping vigil on my forehead as I suffered a protracted migraine. I was struggling for a solution that wouldn't end my exchange outright. I didn't want to surrender my commitment as Frau Hallberg. I'd come such a long way.

At the same time, I'd also become the teacher I never wanted to be: Bitter. Exhausted. Victimized. Overextended and taken for granted. Never present with anyone, let alone myself, except when throbbing migraines landed me in bed and I couldn't escape. What good was I to the world if I never experienced joy? Or worse—if I were dead?

With no solution in sight, I surrendered to sleep . . .

Finally, after several days, the grinding pain had started to lift. I gingerly opened my carry-on and started pulling out souvenirs. A fridge magnet with a quote from Goethe read, *You must do what you cannot leave alone.* And that was mother my children. Also take better care of myself.

I sat at my desk and turned on my computer. "Dear Julia and Sabine,"

I typed, "I'm sorry. I can't continue the exchange."

When I finished the letter, I sent another to parents and students already recruited for a future exchange. "My own children are growing up so fast . . ."

As soon as I hit send, my headache loosened its grip.

&

A postcard of Goethe's color wheel arrived the next day. The energy swirled through my head, yellow, green, blue, indigo, fuchsia, orange. I took in Eva's beautiful, jaunty script.

Dear Amy!

In the past days I have thought of you often and been so happy that we have seen each other again. Last week I was at a Goethe lecture and had to think of you.

Such loving greetings,

Your Eva

Her message recalled the final stanza of Goethe's "Welcome and Farewell":

I went, you stood and looked toward earth

And watched me go with teary eyes.

And yet what joy, to be beloved!

And loving, o gods, what a joy.

Over the next few days, my daughters and I found three gingko trees: one by our local Target, another near a coffee house we liked, and a third outside our church. I took each sighting as a joyous sign.

I'd made the right choice.

◇

"You may find your horizons suddenly broadened," read my fortune cookie from Chinese takeout I ate with my dad the day his mother died. Mere weeks after I quit the exchange, the symbolism didn't escape me. After a rapid decline, Grandma had found her way home. I was seeking another path, one that wouldn't kill me. I'd just started the 2011–2012 school year on a teaching schedule even more ridiculous than the last.

Mom called to tell me about Grandma's passing during my drive between schools, on the third day of classes. I taught at East that day wearing sunglasses to hide my eyes. I took one day off for the funeral. The cheerlessness weighed on me into the fall. I became the mom who said "I told you so" when Olivia fell off the monkey bars and broke her arm. I barked orders to students who barely pretended to listen. Frustration surged through my veins and I saw no end in sight. But I kept praying.

The news that I was leaving German came quietly, a few weeks shy of Christmas. Middle school principals had announced a plan to eliminate exploratory world language classes in seventh grade. The colleague who told me barely spoke above a whisper, but I knew at once when I heard it: after three years of waiting for this particular shoe to drop, here was my miracle.

The following day, I visited the colleague who taught those middle school classes, along with the German One she'd taken over at West. She sat behind her classroom computer, pale red hair pulled into a bun.

"Did you hear the news?" I said. "Without exploratory, you'll teach German full time next year. I'll move over to Spanish."

She looked up at me, one eye green and the other blue. "You don't know that."

I held her gaze, surprisingly comforted by this woman whose presence in the district had once posed such a threat. She even had her own exchange, to Bavaria. I'd hosted her German visitors in my classes for years.

"There's no other option," I said, entirely grounded. "I know how many students we have in the spring, how many return to German each fall. That's one full-time position. You deserve a job."

"I've seen many changes," she said. "We'll have to wait and see."

"I know what I know." I put my hand on her shoulder. "I get to wrap up my work and say goodbye."

She smiled slightly.

I turned to go but stopped at the doorway. "Julia wants to bring one last group from Karlsruhe. Will you host them if I make arrangements?"

"Of course."

❧

I had no idea where I'd end up the following year. Meanwhile, I focused on German. Call it my swan song and final curtain. All through that winter, I made those classes count while keeping my chin up in Spanish One. By spring break 2012, I was anxious for a sign.

Spring erupted in Minnesota while my family was away, skiing in the mountains as guests of Dave's dad. When we pulled into our driveway, I pointed out a nest tucked into the transom above our front door. The girls cheered. On the doorstep, we found a neat pile of grass not yet woven in. Surely the absent mother hadn't laid her eggs yet. The image came straight from my beloved *Demian*. Hesse's words flooded over me. *"Der Vogel kämpft sich aus dem Ei."*—The bird fights its way out of the egg. To experience new beginnings, you have to break out of shells that once protected you. "*Der Vogel fliegt zu Gott.*" Released, the bird flies to God and lives new dreams.

"It can't stay there," Dave said, rubbing his head.

"It can't?"

"How will people come inside? Baby birds won't survive if their mother has to leave."

Mira launched into a chorus of pleas. Olivia took a deep breath and looked her father in the eye. "The babies will be OK."

I understood Dave's problem, but I'd already taken their side. We abandoned the nest to tend to suitcases, going in through the garage. When I snuck into our yard, I heard the flutter of wings and saw a streak of rusty feathers. The mother—a robin redbreast—sat in the tree keeping watch. Across the street, a blue jay perched on a mailbox tweeted. A single goose honked as it passed overhead.

The birds flew as free as . . . well, birds. We had no business stopping them.

I went and stood in front of Dave. "I want the nest above the door."

"Okay." He seemed relieved.

From inside our house, I watched shadows through frosted glass. Porch light by night, sunlight by day revealed the mother bird's profile. Her motionless head rose, and tail feathers jutted out behind her. She'd kept her vigil for days. Meanwhile, my courage had surged and wavered. I was an overgrown bird, trapped inside my too-small world. Or was I the egg?

At work, I pieced together information from snippets of conversation. To create a full-time position for me at East High, administrators could grant the voluntary extension of a Spanish colleague's parenting leave. Or, they could let go of a talented young Spanish teacher everyone loved and give me her position. I couldn't let myself think about that. They promised my move out of German would only last one year, and then everything would return to normal, but I didn't believe it.

Before bed, standing in my darkened hallway, I saw shadowy wishes play out. Little wings unfolded. Bobbling heads reached to take worms. I let myself believe that nobody else needed to lose for me to win.

One day, I forgot and put Wolfgang on a leash, going out through the front door. Across the street, a neighbor's dog began to bark, and I turned to see the babies frozen in position, mouths agape, round eyes unmoving. They weren't ready to fly yet, but soon.

On another day, a Saturday, I made plans with a neighbor to bring our girls to a farmer's market. She said she would pick us up. I didn't expect her to ring the doorbell, and when I opened the door, I didn't expect the horrified look on her face. On the cement, one large baby bird lay crumpled at her feet. It had fully feathered wings, and its eyes showed life. It was breathing heavily, twiglike yellow legs curled into its body.

"I didn't mean to startle the mother," my friend said. "I was thinking you must enjoy all that bird poop. When I looked down, there was the baby."

"Do you think it's hurt?" I felt my heart tighten.

"Let's close the door and let it be," said my friend.

We shuffled my girls out the door. From the car, I called Dave to warn him. And I forgot to worry. An hour later, we were headed for home when Dave called.

"The bird's still there," he said. "It hasn't moved."

*That's not how this story goes, though, you see?* The metaphor was about finding safe places to land. Not falling on the front step and dying.

My friend dropped us off at the curb. From the street, we saw nothing. We crept forward, scanning peony shoots for traces of movement. Moving across the lawn, we spotted the fledgling on the concrete slab. It hopped back to the doorframe and tried to fly upward with outstretched wings. My shoulders relaxed. The girls beamed.

The bird wasn't injured. It would fly soon. Its nestmate was hopping around on the transom. Across the street, on a sign designating wetland, the mother stood watch.

Suddenly, the baby took flight. It landed on the gutter next door. We cheered. Giddy, I ran inside to tell Dave and call my friend.

When I returned, the other baby had gone too. The empty nest darkened the window. The mother was still perched on the small metal sign. In the days that followed, I listened for the symphony of birdsong.

And I smiled.

# 22

## Bridging the Gap / Überbrückung

It was official. I was moving to Spanish at East High School. For good. German ideas I'd reworked for years, documents perfected through countless revisions, were arranged in manila folders and computer files to pass on to my successor. Between the two buildings, I'd taught German for seventeen years.

I told anyone who would listen that I was graduating from West High School, donning a robe and walking with students as a line leader in the ceremony. Just to be sure I couldn't back out, I signed up to read names.

Over the weeks leading up to graduation, I recalled the pageantry of that day when my old friend Lisa and I marched side by side. Bathed in June's early-evening sun, Lisa spoke about piecing together the puzzles of our lives. Whereas I stood before the assembled crowd and invoked the Berlin Wall, insisting we must likewise tear down metaphorical walls in our lives. I said we should show courage, but in many ways, I'd built my fortifications higher over the years.

Looking back, it seemed to me I backed away from true vulnerability at every turn before taking on the impossible assignment of ricocheting back and forth between high schools. *Please let me do this unreasonable thing*, I begged my body for three years running: teach six different preps, several levels at a time, two languages, two schools, every day. All year long, my body had said, *Yes, I will.* Until graduation day, when it said, *I'm done.*

Every year during this time, I prayed a simple prayer on the last day of school: *Just let me get home. There's the river. Let me get home. There's my street. I am almost home.* Bolting from my car, my head pounding, my body depleted, I would collapse onto my front step, sitting for countless minutes, staring at the pond. Then I would go inside, crawl into bed to enjoy a dreamless sleep, and decompress in my house for two days. Missing graduation.

Knowing I needed this year's rite of passage, my body responded by crashing on a Friday, two weeks early. In my morning classes, my head ached as if drawn tight by a rubber band, so weary from telling people where I was headed, answering questions, and explaining how I felt. So I called for a sub and texted Dave to pick up the girls. For eleven hours, I sat curled up on a couch, watching mindless TV dramas punctuated by show tunes.

That weekend gave me enough respite to keep going two more weeks.

On the day I wrapped up my final classes at West, my German One students gave me a red rose and asked me once more not to leave. The German Two students, taught the previous year by my colleague, sat stone-faced as I thanked them for their hard work. In Spanish One, kids took a test all hour and we never said goodbye at all.

After they left, I erased my final words from the whiteboard, written in the letters I'd carefully shaped since kindergarten. I piled boxes atop a cart and pulled posters from the walls. Everything I might use again already sat in plastic Ikea tubs at the back of my classroom in East, waiting for a Spanish room to open. When it felt right, I'd presented artifacts to students. To Luke, who started learning German my first year at East and went on my second exchange trip, I'd given a poster of the Karlsruhe pyramid—camel and palm tree superimposed.

I paused over a postcard of polished river stones. One stone read *Liebe.* Another read *Glück*, a third *Vertrauen*, and the last *Mut*. Love, luck, trust, and courage. That one I planned to hang up at home, somewhere I'd see it often.

On top of my load, I balanced the rose and a poster for Jenna, from our first Karlsruhe exchange. It was a panorama of people dancing at the Berlin Wall the day East Germans finally joined the party. *November 9, 1989*, it read. Jenna's mother actually stood in that jubilant crowd. As in, she's pictured there. Whereas I was on the unpainted side of the Wall for less than an entire head-splitting day.

Most of the German lessons I gave had taken place within this building. It was also where I'd perfected my own grammar. When two teachers from Bavaria had visited my classroom earlier that final year, I asked them to look over some questions I'd prepared for my advanced students. I wanted to ask how Germany could bridge cultural differences between former East and West Germans. *"Eine Brücke aufbauen,"* I'd written—To build a bridge.

They spent several minutes discussing my translations. Eventually we settled on more literal words. Still, one of the teachers liked my poetry. "The other is more direct," he said. "But I don't quite want to let this image leave the page."

At the time, I smiled with a self-assurance developed over years.

I didn't quite want the image to leave either. That poetic, playful side of me didn't exist yet in Spanish.

I wheeled the cart out of my classroom and locked the door.

The halls echoed, afternoon light streaming through windows near the ceiling, shadows darkening the locker bays. Two girls sat against the lockers.

"Hola, Profe," said the one from my Spanish class.

I smiled. "Didn't anyone tell you it's summer?"

"I go to East," her friend said. "Aren't you the German teacher there?"

"I used to be," I said, and kept rolling. Outside, I lugged the cart over the curb and across the parking lot. After placing the rose on the passenger seat, I loaded the boxes and pushed the empty cart back into the building.

Returning to my minivan, I saw that a bird—birds?—had dropped blotches of white across the front windshield, the moon roof, and somehow the windows on both sides as well. It reflected the way I felt. Who was I beyond Frau Hallberg?

I set off to retrieve my daughters. Riding in the backseat, they read my silence with precision.

"Why are you sad?" Olivia asked. "It's a good day."

"I'm won't teach German after tomorrow."

"That's not true," Olivia said. "You'll teach German again."

"You can teach us German," Mira said.

As if on command, the gray skies unleashed raindrops on my car, smudging the splattered white spots on the windows. To my right, the sun broke free, close to the horizon in a widening blue patch. And on my left, the arc of a rainbow emerged across the entire sky. The sun showers followed us home, washing my car clean.

⟨✧⟩

The last time I brought a group to the Schwarzwald, I asked Julia if we could drive the bus past the Hirschsprung statue. "I looked for it whenever I went into Freiburg," I told her.

"Yes," Julia said. "I did too."

And so our bus set off into the Höllental Valley, the road far wider than when the stag made his glorious leap. Julia kept watch a seat ahead of me, along with a German girl behind me, ready to signal everyone when the statue came into view.

"Ohhh!" they called out in unison, recoiling.

I spun around. "What happened? Did we miss it?"

"Someone painted the statue," Julia answered. "It's covered in red and green."

The girl sat shaking her head. "I can't believe someone would do that."

⟨✧⟩

As graduation day approached, I couldn't help thinking of that stag. Preparing for my own leap, I was also blemished but still standing. Those dangerous three years had pushed me to the edge, and I'd survived.

As evidence, a roomful of passionate boys and a handful of tenacious girls at East High School brought me a sheet cake, decorated with a German flag. "*Danke, Frau!*" read the neat black letters.

During their presentations, I cut the cake into squares and passed them around. Groups cheerfully explained grammar concepts, and I could barely contain my pride. Somehow I'd taught them how to play with words despite the chaos of recent years.

As a matter of course, I clued students in on my secret: German grammar may be exacting, but within the bounds of this language, I'd learned to let myself fall short of perfection.

"We'll speak Baby Deutsch," I insisted. "Like in kindergarten. We'll be foolish together."

My time in kindergarten actually did provide the model for my teaching style. For example, that compulsion to make my handwriting pretty, even on impromptu whiteboard notes. I was known for having my visual resources laid out just so—all those worksheets and colorful posters and handmade, hands-on signs. And helping students find friends as they learned.

Just before the final bell rang, I gave an impromptu parting speech in a surge of energy. Afterward, I took in the applause, my elation bordering on headache. It was one thing to feel that pull and another to step into what lay ahead. After all, that stag crossed over because he had to.

$\mathcal{O}$

On the evening of graduation, I arrived early at the colossal church in the next town over. My head was still buzzing, so I played a few Comedian Harmonist songs to calm myself. *"Auf Wiedersehen,"* I sang along, before I emerged from my car.

In a back hallway, I gathered the students on my list and reviewed the pronunciation of every name. We double-checked that my hood looked right and their caps sat straight on their heads.

"Stay within the lines! The lines are our friends," I joked, recalling a car commercial from the nineties. It showed small children coloring at their desks while a humorless teacher marched through the aisles. I reassured students that they wouldn't trip.

"On an occasion like this," I gushed, "you can assume something will go wrong. It's your job to spot that thing, fix it if you can, and then laugh at it—aha, that's what it is." But we marched in to the steady rhythm of *Pomp and Circumstance*, our images projected on giant screens as we processed around the auditorium, and nobody tripped, not once.

While the first graduates crossed the stage, I ran through my names silently. When the usher signaled me, I got up to lead my row, advancing to the microphone for my turn. First. Middle. Last. Wait for the other speaker at the other side of the stage, take another card, and read the name written on it. Deposit it facedown in the box on the podium. Easy. Each name perfectly weighted, in measured cadence, with resonance.

After I read the last name I looked up and followed the graduates across the stage. Walking toward the principal, I wondered why he looked puzzled. Smiling, I turned at the stairs in the middle of the stage and stepped down. That's when my error dawned on me: I should've exited a different way.

The kids in my row, after receiving their diplomas and moving their tassels from right to left, had already filled in the row, leaving one empty seat on the far end. My seat.

Not knowing what to do, I kept walking. A voice called from the crowd, "Go sit in the back, Amy!" It had to be a colleague in the audience. I didn't stop until I reached an empty row. When I did, I crossed over, wandered back up the aisle, and sank into my seat.

My deaf friend, who taught American Sign Language, turned around in her chair a few rows up and signed, "Ha-ha! I saw you. You got lost."

I watched how each successive reader slipped off stage, unnoticed, after reading the names. I remembered precious little after that, just sitting in a daze. The ceremony ended, the students tossed their hats, and it was done.

Rachel—from my second exchange—came to get her picture taken with me in the lobby afterward. "Thanks so much, Frau, for the advice," she said. "I was so nervous I would trip on my heels. But I remembered how you said to make a game of it, and I relaxed."

☙

The morning after graduation, I received an email from Eva, and my heart leapt. She was in Berlin, at a conference. "After dinner, we walked through the Brandenburg Gate. I thought of you and wished you were there."

I scrolled down to see its image. *Das Brandenburger Tor.* Where Germany's past and future converged, the four horses of its quadriga dark against a cloudy blue sky, a staff with the Iron Cross, an eagle rising above them. I let myself feel the bittersweet mixture of joy and sadness. I didn't know when I would ever get back there.

I rolled out of bed and wandered into my office, where I dug out a red album edged in gold. I flipped through its yellowed self-stick pages until I reached my graduation portrait, a moody ingénue. From the next page of the scrapbook, Ben and Amy smiled their matching, overly toothy grins. Gold honor cords dangled from her neck. Triumphant, they held the plaque that declared her valedictorian. She'd surpassed him in German, but he never dropped out of Spanish. Decades later, I was still wondering how I'd ever get good enough. Quitting was no longer an option.

I closed the cover and scanned the room. On the carpet in the corner, a thick volume had waited for the school year to end: my journal from West Germany at seventeen.

*Feelings*, proclaimed the rainbow letters across its cover, wandering clouds on a field of blue sky. The embodiment of a seventies lounge song, it catalogued every event, meticulously recorded for just such a time of reflection. With German, my youthful perseverance was rewarded. If I could stomach that journal, I might learn from my past mistakes.

♌

Several weeks into the summer, I worked up my courage and grabbed the Feelings journal. So much had happened since then—and I knew I'd find raw ignorance staring me in the face. And rejection. And opportunities for gratitude lost. I hardly wanted to own it, but there it was. I planned to read myself to sleep. Instead, I grew more alert, unable to look away from my teenaged self.

What can anyone do with that startling vulnerability when language is stripped away? That familiar fear I still dreaded. When I looked up, it was past midnight. My temples buzzed, my mind raced, but I resolved to stay with my younger self through the last entry in 1987.

Just past three in the morning, I closed the back cover and turned out the light. The panicked voices echoed inside my head. *German was hard, but she thinks she's out of the woods, that former self, hopeful on the final page. I know how long of a journey she has ahead, just as trouble surely awaits me now as a Spanish teacher.*

Shortly before sleep overtook me, I realized why the date of the final entry mattered: It was twenty-five years to the day since the younger me had closed the cover and walked on, one day before Eva turned seventeen. That meant it was now Eva's forty-second birthday. And we were no longer together.

She couldn't help me with this. I had to face teaching Spanish alone.

*ℰ*

I awoke to daylight mere hours later with a pit in my stomach, weak and slightly dizzy. When Dave emerged from the man-cave where he fell asleep and I told him what I'd done, he grimaced and rubbed my back. Later, when I called Mom, the tears broke free after months of convincing myself my heart wasn't breaking. They came in waves, washing over and through me.

"The thing is," I told Mom between gasps, "I'm not that good at Spanish."

Mom listened, absorbing my outbursts with intermittent *mmm-hmms*. After a while, she cut me off. "You needed to read it," she said. "But you're not that girl anymore."

"Was I really so pathetic?"

"Courageous," she said. "How many people dare to do what you've done?"

"Maybe," I said. "I quit Spanish when it got hard."

"Did you know my church asked me to be an exchange student, like you and Eva?" Her voice sounded wistful. "We were so poor. I never even considered going." She paused. "You taught yourself Spanish and went to Seville. I think you'll figure it out."

And it was true. At twenty-three, I'd found a language school in *Sevilla*. I paid a family for room and board and fended for myself. My host father, hearing my plans to become a teacher, predicted long years would pass before I ever taught the language.

His wife nodded. "But it wouldn't bother us if you visit again."

I never did return, but that younger Amy got herself all the way to the Alhambra and back again just by following road signs. And when she missed her flight home in Frankfurt, she talked her way onto the last plane bound for New York, imploring the Spanish airline agents in German, English, and Spanish. Rather than wait for a flight to Minnesota, rather than wait for her luggage to catch up, rather than call Eva to rescue her.

It would take months for Amy's nondescript taupe suitcase and its mix of German and Spanish treasures to catch up. But it did turn up. Eventually, everything arrived.

$\mathscr{D}$

My mother always told me I could learn any language I wanted. She spent thousands of dollars sending me to language camps as a kid—first French and then Swedish. For four years running, her entire teacher's salary paid for my undergraduate education.

A few days after reading the journal, I called her from the road.

"Why did you choose French?" I asked. She'd taken French in college, although the professor never once asked her to read aloud in class.

"Oh," she mused. "Well, they said it was a pretty language."

"Why didn't you take Spanish? You can't spell in English. In French, they don't pronounce half the letters. They have those extra fragments. French is hard."

"Is it?" she murmured. "You know, I worked hard. I was proud to earn Bs. My sisters spoke Spanish . . ." She trailed off, then continued in a rush. "I wanted to learn a language where nobody could correct me."

"I've been thinking about it." I dove in. "All those foreign phrases you used to say? None of them were Spanish. You were good at math, like Ben. And you drove us to Minneapolis for math every week during the school year, but Swedish camp in the summer? You never came to get me like other parents. I rode the bus. You picked me up in a parking lot."

"No . . ."

I was drowning in her silence.

For so long I had tried to understand my mom when we'd gone off course, leaving me gasping for breath. I'd had to learn to embrace that scared girl inside who just wanted to know where we stood.

But looking back after years of teaching languages, I see what Mom hid in plain sight. She nurtured in me gifts she didn't possess, pushing me toward dreams she didn't dare imagine for herself.

When she finally spoke, her voice had grown harsh. "No," she said. "I never was good at languages. You were like my sisters."

Hearing her say this, I had no words to thank her. She gathered all the tools she had and offered them to me. Then she sent me out—alone—with a simple set of instructions: Educate yourself.

# PART FOUR

# Nachspiel /
# Postlude

2014

# 23

## Full Circle / Der Kreis schließt sich

We watch the ravens swooping close outside the window. They ride the wind over the city, their warbling cries ringing out, past towering trees we now know as Sitka spruce, red and white cedar, western hemlock. Out over the bay, the birds disappear against the dusky backdrop.

It reminds me of a cross between the Boundary Waters and my favorite German romantic paintings. Except that in Ketchikan, Alaska, it rains constantly, steady droplets intermittent with a pervasive fog that nourishes those trees. A temperate rain forest, the locals remind us. Liquid sunshine.

The waitress delivers our plates just as my parents, my brother, and his family walk into the restaurant.

"Eva!" Ben and I cry in unison, throwing our arms around each other. The greeting hearkens back to that first time I met my future sister-in-law, Sondra, in the summer of 1989, when she drove up with Ben from Chicago. I looked right past them and barreled toward Eva. Ben's greeted me this way ever since.

I turn to hug Sondra; my lookalike niece, Selena, just back from Spain; and my preteen nephew, Jason, who fears me a little. I have been known to make him eat vegetables. Sitting down, I offer Ben a slice of my smoked salmon, capers, and cream cheese on flatbread.

"Oh, no, I couldn't," he says, the way we Minnesotans do so we don't impose.

I offer again, and then a third time.

"Don't mind if I do," he finally says. The ritual comforts me, a reminder of our common roots. It also feels dated. I hand another slice to Dad, who accepts right away.

A family cruise in the Alaskan wilderness, our parents' wish for their fiftieth anniversary, sounded risky: a week adrift on Alaska Time.

To preserve my marriage and my sanity, I passed on the pre-trip through Denali National Park. But my parents made it impossible to refuse the boat itself. Dad forwarded emails detailing our Kids in Nature week with Un-Cruise Adventures—just fifty other passengers and us. Mom delivered rain pants and rubber boots to our front door. Before flying out, they handed us four maroon sweatshirts. *The Hallberg Crew*, they said in large gold letters. Two white boats raced across their fronts, each with a team of five, the captain calling through a megaphone. Dad beamed. "Don't you just love it?"

When we board our boat in the evening, the seas are so rough, the rain pelting us on the gangplank, that the captain waits to set off, to let the storm subside. Sometime in the night, I hear the buzz of the motor and feel the rocking left and right beneath us in bed.

In the morning, we don the rain jackets, rain pants, and rubber boots to go ashore in a tiny village.

"Do you see that raven working so hard up there?"

Our young guide with a full beard stands behind me on the walkway. I note the black wings outspread, the dipping down and the swooping upward. "As breezy as it gets down here, the wind speed is much greater up there. That bird is holding its own."

A man who comes from this village waits in a clearing. He's wearing a bucket hat and navy rain jacket, ready to guide us into the forest. The kids count each slug, puce and white and gray. Finally we stand before a pole in a clearing, aqua and red and black and white, animal faces stacked on each other. The man addresses our circle.

"Some people misunderstand our totem poles." His lyrical tone captivates me. "I can't stop them from misunderstanding. But we don't worship these poles. They're not gods or any religion. They're a way of remembering our stories, stories of who we are and where we've come from, stories we guard and only tell each other. The rings at the top commemorate potlatches, coming together with other communities to witness important events in our lives."

My nephew approaches me on the trail walking back. "Do you like ravens, Aunt Amy?" Jason stares up at me, his face framed by white-blond locks, his smile impish like my brother's at that age, but his blue eyes serious. I nod.

"I saw you watching that one earlier. I like them too," he says, clearly not afraid. "They say dogs are smart, but what's so smart about doing as you're told? That's why I prefer cats. They tell you what they want, and you get it for them. But ravens are smartest of all. They figure out what they want, and they get it for themselves."

*≈*

I set my plate on the table the following day, where my extended family is eating breakfast. "Can we all wear our sweatshirts today and take the Christmas pictures?" I ask. "I've been wearing mine at night. It's starting to show."

"Why are you sleeping in it?" my brother asks, scolding me as if I'm a petulant child.

"Because it's cold with our window open."

"Close the window." He doesn't bother looking up from his plate.

"I like sleeping with it open. Why can't I wear my sweatshirt?"

"I prefer it open," Dave says. "I like breathing the fresh air."

After breakfast, bundling up in our cabin, I let myself feel the energy of this exchange, puzzling over why I can't let old stories go. Everyone's so used to our exchanges they don't bat an eye. It was so much easier when I knew who I was and where I was going. Grabbing my boots in the hall, I meet Sondra, emerging from their room. After years of marriage to Ben, she's an excellent intermediary. And her older brother's brilliant too.

"I'm frustrated about breakfast," I say. "I'm enjoying the trip, but this isn't my speed. I'm here to honor my parents. And it's not Ben's business what I wear."

"Don't worry about it." She smiles and tips her head. "He's not."

On a beach walk later that morning, Dave, Selena, and I wander past mounds of blue mussels clamped onto beds of ochre kelp and taste bright green sea lettuce. I photograph trees, the sea, a boy holding a rusty starfish. Even the rocks below my feet, subtle and iridescent. I pick one up.

"Look at this, Selena."

"That's a good one, Aunt Amy."

"How about this one?" I say, turning another over, weighing it in my hands.

"Nah," she replies, thoughtful. "It's not so unusual."

"I can throw them back later. I just like gathering them."

"That's true," she says. "Then you should keep it."

"I like it here. We can go at our own pace."

"My dad takes forever to leave a museum," Selena says, animated. "And my roommates in Spain! Don't get me started. They spent their whole time partying."

"But did you learn Spanish?"

"Yeah, some."

Dave wanders nearby. Last night, he retrieved me from our cabin, where I was skipping a talk on glaciers. Ben had enjoyed it. Apparently he jumped in to elaborate. The lecture ended abruptly when orcas appeared off the bow. We stood up top to ooh and ahh. Crew members squealed to see whales so close, round and sleek. They linger on my mind.

"Do you think the Loch Ness Monster was a giant whale?"

"No, Aunt Amy. I don't think so."

We meander on the beach until the skiff arrives to retrieve us for lunch.

❧

Talking with other passengers, I've struggled to define myself, even before we broke out those Hallberg sweatshirts. I usually fall back on my work. "This will be my twentieth year as a teacher," I tell anyone who asks. "I taught German for seventeen years." (Saying I teach Spanish feels oversimplified.) More often than not, I've skipped small talk to join Selena below deck, reading my book while she writes pieces of a novel on her laptop.

"Yes, those are our twins," I say when a woman with red hair and her dignified husband join Dave and me at a table during happy hour.

"Is one easier to deal with than the other?" she asks.

"It's hard to explain. They're so different."

"We have identical twin grandsons back home," she says, peering through her glasses. "Have you brought your girls on trips before?"

Dave and I exchange glances, smiling. "We took them to Germany," he says.

It feels like a lifetime ago. While finalizing our Alaska booking, I discovered my passport had expired without me even noticing.

❧

"The thing about Germany," Ben chimes in during a ride to a cave, "is that everyone speaks English. You can't get better at German because they never let you use it."

"Maybe." The bus bumps along on the road. "I got my students speaking. It's made a great niche for several of them."

I don't mention that I've been traveling to his alma mater in Chicago for weekend seminars, halfway to a certificate in German translation. And yes, it became possible because I gave up teaching German. I know my Spanish position is one more step out the door.

I begin working my family connections into all my conversations. "We're celebrating my parents' fiftieth anniversary. You've probably met my brother, the professor." When a younger kid can't quite keep up with the older ones on our river walk, I say, "That's the story of my life. I was the little sister. It's hard."

The day our whole family goes out in kayaks, Olivia and I fall behind from the start.

"The boat's right there," I say in desperation. "We can follow the group or go back to the boat. Make up your mind."

"I don't want to go back," she moans.

"Then let's call out strokes."

"Left, right, left, right," she sings. It makes its own harmony. After a while, I add a wandering melody. "Jellyfish," I call out at intervals.

"Where? Oh, there." After a while, she sings in German, "*Links, rechts, links, rechts. Vorwärts, nicht hinten.*" Forward, not backward.

My parents have fallen back to wait for us. The rest of the group circles an island, killing time until we catch up. Dave and Mira set off once the boat comes back into view.

"Do you see the boat?" I ask the flagging Olivia. "Let's count twenty strokes at a time and see how quickly we get there." My arms burn, but we dig in, counting to twenty, then thirty, then forty. Our simple song carries us all the way home.

We've almost reached the last open spot at the docking station when Ben and Selena pull ahead.

"Can you let us win just this once," I say, "when we really need it?" And without a word, my brother lets us pass.

❧

In the evening, all the passengers travel by skiff to an island beach. The air feels balmy as I scan the smooth rocks.

I ask the bearded guide about deciduous trees on the forest border.

He sits on a log, doling out marshmallows for kids to toast in the fire.

"You ask the best questions," he says. "So remember that this landscape is always changing, rising up, the forest evolving. Deciduous trees grow fast. The evergreens catch up through persistence."

The sky turns vibrant colors. While Dave and I wait for the next skiff, our girls and some other kids stand on a rugged black outcropping. I climb up after them.

"Look." Olivia points to a tide pool. "It's an anemone."

"Do you think," I ask, "since this land is always rising up, that we are standing, right now, at the summit of a future mountain?" For the benefit of another mother nearby, I add, "I'm not a scientist, so I can ask these foolish questions."

"Pardon?" she says. Her son has played with my nephew all week.

"I'm the stupid younger sister, you see. My brother's the professor." It's an old, favorite joke of mine.

The woman tips her head. "I'm not sure I know who that is."

"He's Jason's dad," I say.

Her mouth makes a small o. I hear her speak to her son as I walk away. "We won't have that problem, because your sister is not stupid."

I turn around. "No, see, I'm not stupid, I'm actually smart. That's the joke."

She stares at me. I walk back to the pile of life jackets and grab one, mumbling, "What is wrong with me?"

Watching the skiff approach, I recount the conversation to my sister-in-law. "It was mortifying. I have to stop telling that story."

Sondra shakes her head. "I used to go on about my bad experiences in high school. Then my corporate coach asked me to step outside my comfort zone. So I went to my reunion."

"And how'd that go?"

She nods. "It went alright."

*⊘*

Our family of ten sets out the next morning in the skiff, along with a driver and the resident glacier guy who spoke earlier in the week. Bundled up, we edge ever closer to the wall of ice. Large chunks of ice infused with a blue glow float all around us.

Ahead of us, a jagged wall of blue ice streaked with soil deposits seals off the fjord.

"I saw it calve earlier this morning," Ben tells us. "It could happen again at any time."

"That's why we stay back," our driver says. Still, she edges us forward. Here and there, seals pop their heads up among the bobbing ice. I only half listen, grasping Olivia after making her keep her feet under the safety cord.

"Why would the seals like it in here?" our guide asks.

"To stay away from the whales," Jason answers.

"Right. And their necks are fused, so they peek up like little periscopes," says my brother. He turns and gestures toward the murky gray water. "The portion of the ice that we see is just a fraction of the portion underwater. Do you know why the ice is so blue?"

We lean forward, waiting for him to answer his own question.

"Because it's been under such pressure for thousands of years, kind of like a diamond, that the crystal structure at its core is incredibly compact. That creates that blue color."

A crack rings out like a gunshot. A minute later, a small chunk falls away, landing at the base of the wall. We keep watching. Then, all in an instant, a large slab of ice falls from the glacial face, splintering into fragments below. A cold breeze sweeps over us, sending waves radiating from the sheet of ice.

Back on the boat, the barkeep greets us with cocoa and peppermint schnapps my brother won't drink because he doesn't like chocolate. Instead he stands on the deck for a few hours, waiting and watching the giant ice shed layers into the freezing water below. Dave joins him, and later the girls, for as long as the glacier stays in sight.

But not me.

The numbness I felt earlier in the trip, the wish to connect with my brother at a meaningful level—heck, at any level—has given way. After lunch, I retreat to our cabin, sprawling across the bed. Hot tears spill across my cheeks. I take out some paper and begin writing. All trip long, I've spotted him talking to other people, sharing his knowledge, seen them listen intently. I've had decent conversations myself. I just want something different from my brother, a connection not already scripted. And he's not comparing himself to me. He's mostly left me alone, which I've asked for all along.

I wipe my tears when Dave opens the door. "Are you OK?" he asks, taking me in.

"I'm so angry at Ben, but I'm expecting him to be someone he's not. I want him to care what I think. I know a lot about the topics the guides are discussing."

"But that's not ever who he was," Dave says, even-keeled.

"Right. I'm making it harder than it has to be."

"Do you want to go kayaking?" he asks.

"Let's go kayaking."

$\mathscr{O}$

They launch us from the boat and we glide across the opaque waters of a much warmer bay near the glacier. After the hard pulls with Olivia and the resulting ache in my arms, I find it surprisingly easy to paddle with Dave steering. We paddle, then stop to coast beneath a cloudless blue sky.

We stroke gently, left-right, gliding toward two parallel waterfalls. One marches its jaunty path down barren rock face. The other meanders, tripping down rocks, veering off through surrounding greens. Both spill inexorably into the opaque water below, grayish green from glacial till, suspended pulverized sediment. Over toward the edges, the silt has begun to disperse, taking on an aqua hue. I can hear a rushing sound, amplified louder than either waterfall could make alone.

A question arises: Must there be only two options? Yes or no? German or Spanish, before or after, West or East, right or wrong, right, left, *rechts, links*? I've never thought in terms of Mira or Olivia. Why exactly Ben or Amy, two versions of truth?

Family doesn't work that way. And if not two, then how many?

I'm still solving for X, as if all past, present, and future struggles could be resolved through mathematical proofs. As if I can find that magic number X and locate myself.

Seventeen, my age when I first saw Germany and the number of years I taught German.

Sixteen, my age when Ben left home and Eva came to live with us.

Fifteen, the number of years since I met Dave.

Twelve, the number of years Ben lived in our hometown. And the number of years I've lived anywhere else.

Whose are these old parameters? Only mine.

Another number surfaces. Forty-one, the number of years Germany was divided into two lands. And what came before that? Even before the Holocaust, generations of trauma, much of it unspeakable, same as in my homeland. It all happened.

But people can heal. We evolve.

I lived with my brother for such a short time, so long ago. If I let myself stay trapped in old patterns, whose fault is that?

We're together now.

I land on a third option: What if I could honor our common past, admire my brother's genius, and welcome the person I'm becoming? It's time for accepting myself, beyond my idealized fairytale endings. Coming to terms with what is. And forgiveness.

We trace a small circle in the space between the falls. Dave speaks at last. "Do you want to go in or paddle to the other side?"

The air is fresh, the sun warm, the water cool. "Let's paddle on."

Behind rocks and trees, brooks babble in each small cove we pass. Southeast Alaska is covered with them.

The woman with twin grandchildren stands on deck when we return. "How was it?"

"Gorgeous," I reply.

Returning to our sundrenched cabin, I choose forty-one rocks to bring home, one for each year East and West Germany existed before the Berlin Wall fell. It seems like a proper reminder that division comes from within. I scoop the rest into a paper bag and carry them to the top deck. The little ones make a high-pitched *plink*, the larger ones a deeper *splosh*. I toss every last stone into the unfathomable sea. And then I sit and relax.

"Thank you for coming on this trip," Mom says, settling into the chair beside me. She looks out at the ocean while I read.

After a while Selena joins us.

"We've had such fun together, haven't we?" Mom says.

Selena's face brightens.

"You should see what Amy has done with her house." Mom adds. "The girls wanted their own rooms, so Amy turned their playroom into her writer's studio. It's wonderful."

It's true. I have postcards and books and artifacts from all my various travels in there. Somehow it all tells a worthwhile tale. I've gone away, and I've returned.

"You know," I say to my niece, whose serious expression looks so much like my own, "you can call me anytime you want help with Spanish. That's what I teach, you know. I'm pretty good at it."

"Thanks. I will."

🖐

Back in Juneau, ravens flit between trees. Atop a mountain, my brother pours water from his bottle into the open mouths of my children, lifted toward the sun. While Ben and his son continue onward, the rest of us wander through town.

"What do you want to do before you die?" reads a large chalkboard along the street.

I grab some green chalk. "I want to write my story."

# Acknowledgments

If you're part of my life, consider yourself part of this book. I'm grateful to and for you ALL, whether or not you appear in these pages. I've related details as truthfully as I remember. And. I translated true-life events into stories from my perspective.

To make that clear, I've changed names, with few exceptions. When I emailed Eva, asking what I should call her, she replied immediately: "My name is Eva. Any questions?" Thanks for your faith in me.

Mom was wary about letting me host an exchange student, but she's never regretted it. It's been a similar test to watch me write my book. Thank you for your love.

To my dad—thanks for taking us on adventures.

To my brother—thanks for an education like no other.

Remembering my grandparents and aunt—we non-Native peoples are all children of immigrants. You blessed me with that context.

To my daughters—thank you for being yourselves.

Dave, you bought me books on how to write books. As usual, you provided gifts I never knew I always wanted.

I love you ALL.

Deepest thanks to teachers who fed my spirit: Julie Klassen, Richard Cantwell, Arlys Johnson, Julie Albers, Ron Lachelt, Nadja Krämer, Evelyn Meyer, Barbara Cameron, and David & Linda Johnson.

Elizabeth Gilbert: My mother-in-law handed me *Eat Pray Love* as I boarded a plane for Germany. By our return, I'd highlighted passages in multiple colors throughout. Grateful to you for the spark.

The Loft Literary Center at Open Book is a Minneapolis treasure, providing access to real working writers who teach invaluable lessons. Most notably:

Elizabeth Jarrett-Andrew: Thank you for opening door after door.

Cheri Register: Few first-time writers enjoy the ongoing privilege of discussing narrative craft over coffee with the winner of one (now two) Minnesota Book Awards. To win Cheri's respect was a genuine prize.

So much of this work saw its genesis in partnership with my Foreword peers, especially Katherine Quie.

Mary Carroll Moore: Thanks for pulling back the curtain on so many levels, and for pairing me with three writers who profoundly shaped my work, Amy Hanson, Susan Thomas, and Jean Hey.

Heartfelt thanks to the kind souls who read drafts: Jen Bellmont, Judy Stinson, Keri Mangis, Lisa Wald, Ally Bishop, Susan Schierts, and my editor, Anitra Budd.

Thanks also to Christi Sutphen, Kiki Kelley, Anna Hazenberg, Allyson Scammell, Ray DePaola, Sarah Bamford Seidelmann, Rebecca Tolin, and Steph Lagana for essential support.

There's nobody finer than Amy Quale, Roseanne Cheng, and Patrick Maloney at Wise Ink. Thank you for sharing my vision.

# German Awakening

In loving memory of Sophie & Hans Scholl, Friedrich Schiller, and Johann Wolfgang von Goethe. Your light still shines.